Sovereignism and Populism

At a time when populism and appeal for national and popular sovereignty are on the rise – in Europe, the USA, and beyond – this volume proposes a new research agenda in political science that focuses on the linkages between populist and sovereignism in Europe.

The book's core question is to know and describe whether, how, and to what extent populism has been able to articulate the calls for 'taking back control' of the national borders and authority, by looking at both the 'demand' and 'supply' sides. Through compelling empirical analyses, the authors offer fresh data and theoretical insights on the determinants of the support for sovereigntist claims and its impact on voting choices, as well as on the features of the sovereignist discourse in populist parties.

Coupled with the growing electoral success of party-based populism, sovereignism actually poses challenges to the ongoing processes of supranational integration. This urges a timely rethinking of democratic politics and calls for far-sighted alternatives to 'taking back control' to address the impact of globalisation and regionalisation on contemporary societies.

The chapters in this book were originally published as a special issue of the journal, *European Politics and Society*.

Linda Basile is Research Fellow at the Department of Social, Political, and Cognitive Sciences of the University of Siena, Italy.

Oscar Mazzoleni is Professor in Political Science and Director of the Research Observatory of Regional Politics at the University of Lausanne, Switzerland.

Sovereignism and Populism

Citizens, Voters and Parties in Western European Democracies

**Edited by
Linda Basile and Oscar Mazzoleni**

LONDON AND NEW YORK

First published 2022
by Routledge
2 Park Square, Milton Park, Abingdon, Oxon, OX14 4RN

and by Routledge
605 Third Avenue, New York, NY 10158

Routledge is an imprint of the Taylor & Francis Group, an informa business

Introduction, Chapters 2-5, Conclusions © 2022 Taylor & Francis

Chapter 1 © 2019 Reinhard Heinisch, Annika Werner and Fabian Habersack.
Originally published as Open Access.

With the exception of Chapter 1, no part of this book may be reprinted or reproduced or utilised in any form or by any electronic, mechanical, or other means, now known or hereafter invented, including photocopying and recording, or in any information storage or retrieval system, without permission in writing from the publishers. For details on the rights for Chapter 1, please see the chapter's Open Access footnote.

Trademark notice: Product or corporate names may be trademarks or registered trademarks, and are used only for identification and explanation without intent to infringe.

British Library Cataloguing-in-Publication Data
A catalogue record for this book is available from the British Library

ISBN13: 978-1-032-14814-4 (hbk)
ISBN13: 978-1-032-14815-1 (pbk)
ISBN13: 978-1-003-24125-6 (ebk)

DOI: 10.4324/9781003241256

Typeset in Myriad Pro
by codeMantra

Publisher's Note
The publisher accepts responsibility for any inconsistencies that may have arisen during the conversion of this book from journal articles to book chapters, namely the inclusion of journal terminology.

Disclaimer
Every effort has been made to contact copyright holders for their permission to reprint material in this book. The publishers would be grateful to hear from any copyright holder who is not here acknowledged and will undertake to rectify any errors or omissions in future editions of this book.

Contents

Citation Information   vi
Notes on Contributors   viii
Preface   ix
Linda Basile and Oscar Mazzoleni

Introduction: Sovereignist wine in populist bottles?   1
Linda Basile and Oscar Mazzoleni

1   Reclaiming national sovereignty: the case of the conservatives
and the far right in Austria   13
Reinhard Heinisch, Annika Werner and Fabian Habersack

2   Should we stay or should we join? 30 years of Sovereignism and direct
democracy in Switzerland   32
Sean Mueller and Anja Heidelberger

3   Economic populism and sovereignism: the economic supply of European
radical right-wing populist parties   52
Gilles Ivaldi and Oscar Mazzoleni

4   Taking back control? Brexit, sovereignism and populism in
Westminster (2015–17)   69
Gianfranco Baldini, Edoardo Bressanelli and Stella Gianfreda

5   'For whom the sovereignist bell tolls?' Individual determinants of support
for sovereignism in ten European countries   85
Linda Basile, Rossella Borri and Luca Verzichelli

Conclusions. The populism-sovereignism linkage: findings, theoretical
implications and a new research agenda   108
Luca Verzichelli

Index   121

Citation Information

The following chapters were originally published in the journal, *European Politics and Society*, volume 21, issue 2 (2020). When citing this material, please use the original page numbering for each article, as follows:

Introduction
Sovereignist wine in populist bottles?
Linda Basile and Oscar Mazzoleni
European Politics and Society, volume 21, issue 2 (2020) pp. 151–162

Chapter 1
Reclaiming national sovereignty: the case of the conservatives and the far right in Austria
Reinhard Heinisch, Annika Werner and Fabian Habersack
European Politics and Society, volume 21, issue 2 (2020) pp. 163–181

Chapter 2
Should we stay or should we join? 30 years of Sovereignism and direct democracy in Switzerland
Sean Mueller and Anja Heidelberger
European Politics and Society, volume 21, issue 2 (2020) pp. 182–201

Chapter 3
Economic populism and sovereignism: the economic supply of European radical right-wing populist parties
Gilles Ivaldi and Oscar Mazzoleni
European Politics and Society, volume 21, issue 2 (2020) pp. 202–218

Chapter 4
Taking back control? Brexit, sovereignism and populism in Westminster (2015–17)
Gianfranco Baldini, Edoardo Bressanelli and Stella Gianfreda
European Politics and Society, volume 21, issue 2 (2020) pp. 219–234

Chapter 5
'For whom the sovereignist bell tolls?' Individual determinants of support for sovereignism in ten European countries
Linda Basile, Rossella Borri and Luca Verzichelli
European Politics and Society, volume 21, issue 2 (2020) pp. 235–257

Conclusions

Conclusions. The populism-sovereignism linkage: findings, theoretical implications and a new research agenda
Luca Verzichelli
European Politics and Society, volume 21, issue 2 (2020) pp. 258–270

For any permission-related enquiries please visit:
http://www.tandfonline.com/page/help/permissions

Notes on Contributors

Gianfranco Baldini Dipartimento di Scienze politiche e sociali, University of Bologna, Italy.

Linda Basile Department of Social, Political and Cognitive Sciences, University of Siena, Italy.

Rossella Borri Department of Social, Political and Cognitive Sciences, CIRCaP, University of Siena, Italy.

Edoardo Bressanelli Department of European and International Studies, King's College, London, UK.

Stella Gianfreda Institute of Law, Politics and Development, School of Advanced Studies Sant'Anna, Pisa, Italy.

Fabian Habersack Department of Political Science, University of Salzburg, Austria.

Anja Heidelberger Institute of Political Science, University of Bern, Switzerland.

Reinhard Heinisch Department of Political Science, University of Salzburg, Austria.

Gilles Ivaldi URMIS-Université de Nice-Sophia Antipolis, Nice, France.

Oscar Mazzoleni Institute of Political Studies, University of Lausanne, Switzerland.

Sean Mueller Institute of Political Science, University of Berne, Switzerland.

Luca Verzichelli Department of Social, Political and Cognitive Sciences, CIRCaP, University of Siena, Italy.

Annika Werner School of Politics and International Relations, Australian National University, Canberra, Australia.

Preface

By Linda Basile and Oscar Mazzoleni

This book originates from a workshop organised by the University of Lausanne, in collaboration with the University of Siena, held in Lausanne on 10th and 11th November 2017. At that time, Western democracies were experiencing a profound political upheaval. Donald Trump's victory at the US Presidential elections and the Brexit referendum in the UK were just two of the main political events in 2016 that have shaken the world and raised questions and concerns about the likely consequences of this "new turn" in politics.

Such apparently disconnected events, indeed, had common and surprisingly important traits, which are unveiled by the political discourses of their key protagonists. In a speech delivered at the United Nations General Assembly on 19th September 2017, the newly elected President Donald Trump claimed: "… We do expect all nations to uphold these two core sovereign duties: to respect the interests of their own people and the rights of every other sovereign nation. This is the beautiful vision of this institution, and this is foundation for cooperation and success. (…) Strong, sovereign nations let their people take ownership of the future and control their own destiny. And strong, sovereign nations allow individuals to flourish in the fullness of the life intended by God. (…) As President of the United States, *I will always put America first*, just like you, as the leaders of your countries will always, and should always, put your countries first. All responsible leaders have an obligation to serve their own citizens, *and the nation-state remains the best vehicle for elevating the human condition*" (emphasis ours). This surprisingly strong appeal to the US retrenchment and to the primacy of the nation-state mirrored similar pleas on the other side of the Atlantic. During the Brexit campaign, in an editorial published in the *Telegraph* on 25th October 2015, the leader of the British party UKIP, Nigel Farage, claimed that "a proud, patriotic country that has control of its borders, represents itself on the world stage and makes its own laws in our own sovereign Parliament" to get support for the Leave option.

The US and UK cases were outstanding example of a political trend that was emerging across Europe, with political movements appealing to the "national people" and the disadvantaged ones against the supranational institutions, the "elites", and the "foreign threat" gaining increasing electoral success. An editorial published on *The Economist* on 30th July 2016 already sought to describe the unfolding of these political trends by raising a provocative question: Is a new conflict between "open" and "closed" people replacing the traditional left-right divide? Is political competition shifting towards a struggle between those who see the opportunities of global interconnectedness and those who feel that foreign and supranational institutions, global trade, and immigrants have significantly encroached the sovereignty of nation-states, thus undermining people's well-being?

PREFACE

Against this backdrop, the Lausanne's workshop offered a unique opportunity to its participants to share and develop ideas, ongoing research projects, and outputs from newly collected data, about the emerging of a new political divide on sovereignty issues. Moreover, the involved scholars inevitably came to grips with the phenomenon of populism, the "elephant in the room" when dealing with these sovereignist turns in politics. Indeed, although sovereigntist claims pre-exist populism, populist parties have sought to address the diffused feelings of insecurity and dissatisfaction among citizens by taking over ideas such as those of popular and national sovereignty. The insightful debate started in Lausanne thus resulted into a motivating scientific collaboration on the conceptualisation and empirical analysis of sovereignism and its linkages with populism, by looking at both the demand and supply sides of the political conflict.

The original research articles originated by this research project were then collected into a special issue, which was eventually published by *European Politics and Society* in 2020 (Volume 21, number 2). Since its early publication in the online format, the special issue has attracted wide interest, thus confirming that the debate on sovereignism and its linkages with populism is still open and lively. The agenda proposed in the Introduction raises compelling questions reflecting the complexity of the current challenges linking populism and sovereignism, while the research articles included offer a range of methodological approaches, indicators, and theoretical insights that valuably enrich this open-ended debate.

The publication of this special issue into a book confirms the enduring interests of researchers, scholars, as well as of a broader audience to sovereignism and populism in contemporary politics. We are particularly grateful to Routledge for encouraging us to turn the special issue into a book. We believe this will contribute to expand the outreach of this stimulating research project and keep the attention high on the research questions it raises.

INTRODUCTION

Sovereignist wine in populist bottles?

Linda Basile ⓘ and Oscar Mazzoleni ⓘ

ABSTRACT
Sovereignist claims are on the rise – in Europe, the USA, and beyond. In dealing with processes such as globalization and supranational integration, which have progressively shifted powers and competencies away from nation states, these transformations have created a fertile terrain for reactions against the sources of such insecurity, which find full expression in the sovereignist claims to 'take back control', that is to say to return to the traditional understanding of sovereignty being based upon mutually exclusive territories. These sources of insecurity and social unrest have also provided structures of political opportunity for the electoral success of populist parties. Despite its relevance for the understanding of the populist discourse, however, sovereignty has been largely under-theorised by scholars dealing with populism. Accordingly, we propose a new research agenda to study populist mobilization that focuses on the linkage between populism and sovereignism, while also encouraging further theoretical and empirical studies, focusing on both the demand side and the supply side. In particular, we suggest some crucial aspects with which the Special Issue seeks to engage, before pointing to some substantial implications that are likely to emerge from the findings of this research agenda.

1. Introduction

In recent decades, across Europe as well as on the other side of the Atlantic, several actors labelled as populist have achieved significant electoral results and have even succeeded in coming to power by appealing to the 'national people' and the 'disadvantaged', as opposed to supranational institutions, the EU, the global economy, the 'elites', and the 'foreign threat'. (Akkerman, Mudde, & Zaslove, 2014; Kriesi et al., 2012; Mudde, 2007; Wolinetz & Zaslove, 2018). Despite their intrinsic heterogeneity, these parties share a common emphasis on claims of popular sovereignty (De Spiegeleire et al., 2017), as well as 'the belief in the uncontested primacy of national-level politics and the call to recover at this precise level (institutionally as well as territorially) power that has slipped away to more distant and diffuse layers of governance', namely *sovereignism* (Kallis, 2018, p. 299). The seemingly recurrent reference to sovereignism in the populist discourse raises two questions: How do populism and sovereignism relate to each other? Could sovereignism be adopted as a notion to better grasp the nature of populist mobilization?

In this contribution, we will seek to address these questions, while suggesting theoretically grounded insights for a research agenda that explores the linkages between sovereignism and populism. It is organized as follows: In the first and second sections, respectively, we will examine the concept of sovereignty and the current socio-political challenges to nation-states on which sovereignist claims rely. These will provide, in the third section, the theoretical underpinnings regarding the relationship between sovereignism and populism; we will then propose, in the fourth section, a number of issues for a new research agenda aimed at addressing such a close relationship. In the final section, we will briefly introduce the papers included in the present Special Issue, which, by adopting different perspectives and methodological approaches, provide a valuable theoretical and analytical contribution to the development of such a research agenda.

2. Sovereignty: from the modern-state's conceptualization to the contemporary transformations

Sovereignty is an old, yet changing and constantly evolving concept. Alongside the concept of sovereignism, it has long been addressed by several disciplines, including legal studies, political theory, geography, and international relations; in political science, on the other hand, sovereignty has often been considered as a proxy for Westphalian state, or nation-state institutional authority (Keating, 2003, pp. 191–193). Indeed, although the origins of this term can be traced back to ancient Greece and Rome, it was only with the advent of the modern state in the sixteenth century that it developed into the definition of 'full decision-making and authority of a governing body over a clearly defined territory, or a *polity*'. Yet while Bodin and Hobbes conceived of sovereignty as the absolute decision-making power of the ruler (i.e. the king), from Rousseau onwards it became 'the will of the people', which exerts such a power through its representatives (Held, 1995; Sassen, 1996; 2008). The contemporary conceptualization of sovereignty therefore points to at least three core elements: First, sovereignty is exerted over *mutually exclusive territories*, which mostly coincide with the national state; second, it is an expression of the *popular will*; third, such popular will is expressed through *mechanisms of representative democracy,* on which liberal democracies rely.

However, the social, economic, and political processes unfolding since the aftermath of World War 2 and, above all, the fall of the Berlin wall in 1989, have jeopardized such cornerstones of modern sovereignty in contemporary democracies. As some scholars have pointed out, the European nation-states that emerged as core units of the international system within the Westphalian paradigm and were consolidated throughout the nineteenth and early twentieth century, have gradually weakened their sovereignty (Sassen, 2008; Van Creveld, 1999), as a result of the rise and strengthening of supranational and subnational political institutions and transnational corporations, especially in recent decades (Grimm, 2015, pp. 84 ff.; Sassen, 2008, p. 2; Strange, 1996).

Globalized economy and increasing patterns of shared authority, often expressed by forms of supranational integration, have progressively de-territorialized the geography of power, with state economies nowadays required to face complex challenges related to the free movement of capital, the reduction of trade barriers, and the increase of foreign investments; likewise, international conventions and agreements have limited states' control of their borders and of immigration. While globalization has increased states' competencies, the increasing flow of information and of people across borders has challenged 'one of the fundamental principles' of state sovereignty, that is, 'the ability to control what crosses borders' and, more generally, to find at the national level the capacity to adequately answer global problems (Sassen, 1996; 2008). The process of European integration provides a paradigmatic example of this transformation and dispersion of sovereignty away from, but not excluding the national state. This is the case, for instance, with the tension between intergovernmental and supranational institutions in the EU, or the multi-level governance system (Agnew, 2009, p. 97 ff.; Hooghe & Marks, 2003).

These ongoing and relentless processes have not led, however, to a definitive demise of the nation state (Mann, 1997; Smith, Solinger, & Topik, 1999). Rather, sovereignty has been transformed and dispersed across several institutional arenas, with nation-states required to share their decision-making authority with other institutional arenas. This new form of 'diffuse sovereignty' has therefore upended the traditional understanding of sovereignty, based upon the principle of 'mutually exclusive territories' and the modern theory of the liberal democratic state as based on a 'national community of fate [...], which rightly governs itself and determines its own future' (Held & McGrew, 1993, p. 264; Kallis, 2018).

3. From sovereignty to sovereignist claims

All these transformations did not come without consequences. In the early 1990s, Held and McGrew (1993, pp. 284–285) warned that in an increasingly globalizing and regionalizing context, 'the meaning and the place of democratic politics have to be rethought'. They pointed out the urgent need to address the weakened regulatory capacity of nation-states, the challenges to the accountability and representativeness of the democratic states, and the interlocking of political decisions and outcomes across states, as a result of these processes of global interconnectedness: 'If [democratic politics] fails to [come to terms with all these developments], it is likely to become ever less effective in determining the shape and limits of political activity'. (Ibid.) However, more than 25 years later, while national governments have sought over time to develop forms of cooperation and integration in order to better face global challenges, there are significant signs of failure in such attempts at 'rethinking'.

Recent critical junctures have further brought to light the trade-offs and uncertainties related to this shift of sovereignty away from the nation-state. In turn, these uncertainties are likely to trigger a 'societal malaise' (Aschauer, 2017), which represents a fertile terrain for reactions against the sources of such insecurity. For instance, the uprisings in the Arab world, the armed conflict taking place in Syria, and political instability in Libya and other North African countries (Attinà, 2016) have revealed the difficulties in defining effective, coordinated responses at supranational levels. Similarly, when facing the flow of migrants towards their borders, the governments of the European Union have been unable to find a shared agreement on asylum mechanisms and quota-based systems for the relocation of migrants. The global financial crisis, on the other hand, has shown how economic globalization is likely to pose a serious threat to jobs and welfare, while the austerity policies promoted by the EU to address the financial crisis have further exacerbated socio-economic inequalities among Europeans.

In other words, the dispersion and de-territorialization of the centres of powers have weakened the decision-making authority of nation-states, as well as their capacity to address people's uncertainties and concerns with effective policies. As a result, there is an increasing dissatisfaction and lack of trust towards the supranational actors and institutions, which are seen as distant and incapable of effectively addressing the main challenges posed by multi-level governance and the new global order (Dahlberg & Linde, 2016).

Moreover, the evolution of decision-making processes towards multi-level models of governance has raised issues concerning popular legitimacy, democratic accountability, and control over the government (Held, 1995; Keating, 2003; Papadopoulos, 2010). Indeed, with the *loci of power* so territorially dispersed, it is increasingly difficult for ordinary citizens to clearly identify the actors responsible for law-making, or the representatives they could refer to in order to express their complaints or demands. A clear example of the reactions generated by the 'deficit of democracy' and the lack of accountability among the supranational decision-makers are the enduring challenges faced by the process of European integration (Lord & Beetham, 2001; Scharpf, 1999), which reached a peak with Brexit (Clarke, Goodwin, & Whiteley, 2017).

To sum up, as national states have lost their exclusive authority *over their territory*, this has undermined the credibility of national governments, and their elites, to *effectively address* challenges and concerns (i.e. 'to give answers'), *represent the popular will* and act in their interests (i.e. 'to listen to citizens' demands'). It is precisely in this context that reactions to the ongoing transformations of sovereignty arise, thus developing into *sovereignism*, that is, the return to the traditional understanding of sovereignty being based upon mutually exclusive territories and the retrenchment to the national dimension, clearly epitomized by the sovereignist motto: 'take back control' (Kallis, 2018).

4. Bridging sovereignism and populism

The scenario described above has also opened up political opportunities for parties commonly referred to as populist. Despite its growing diffusion, populism is probably one of the current most contested terms in literature and is often used to define even deeply different kinds of actors, ranging from the left to the right of the political continuum. Populism is actually also used to qualify both 'exclusive' and 'inclusive' actors, with the former focusing on identitarian claims rejecting any form of pluralism that might hinder the cultural distinctiveness of the national people, in contrast to the latter. There is little agreement even on the very nature of populism, in terms of it being an ideology, a frame, a political style, or a strategy, as three recently published handbooks show (de la Torre, 2019; Heinisch, Holz-Bacha, & Mazzoleni, 2017; Rovira Kaltwasser, Taggart, & Ostiguy, 2017). Populism is actually a global phenomenon that 'escapes generalization' as 'its language and content are imbued with the political culture of the society in which it arises' (Urbinati, 2019, p. 4). Moreover, when populism is understood as a claim – a discourse or set of attitudes – provided by citizens or political actors to frame the opposition between the 'people' and the 'others' in a Manichean manner, some scholars prefer to use the notion of nationalism (De Cleen, 2017; De Cleen & Stavrakakis, 2017).

Yet, the intrinsic heterogeneity of this group of parties, movements, and leaders should not prevent us from looking for some common denominator that would tie this plurality of *populisms* together and transcend context-based differences. In particular, such a *trait d'union* might be found precisely in the aforementioned concept of sovereignism (Kallis, 2018). Indeed, we might observe that all populist discourses are likely to share appeals to 'the people', while making a claim for a renewed enhancement of national sovereignty. For instance, the leader of the UK Independence Party (UKIP) in Great Britain, Nigel Farage, successfully waved the flag of the 'proud, patriotic country that has control of its borders' in order to get the majority of British votes in favour of the Leave side in the Brexit referendum. In France, Marine Le Pen, the party leader of the Front National (FN), emphasized the fight against the Euro and the need to reduce the power of supranational bodies in her campaign as a candidate for the 2017 French presidency. In Italy, Matteo Salvini led the transformation of the Lega Nord – officially known just as Lega since 2018 – from a regionalist party appealing to Northern Italy, into a nation-based party, waving the motto 'Italians first!' (Albertazzi, Giovannini, & Seddone, 2018; Mazzoleni & Ruzza, 2018). Beyond Europe, the most relevant sovereignist claim emerged in the 2017 election of the US president, Donald Trump, with his slogan 'America first'.

In other words, by addressing the diffuse sense of insecurity among citizens, populist claims for an empowerment of the nation-state are presented to citizens as a way to regain control over the national economy, decision-making and traditions, in the face of globalized flows and supranational powers. As Kallis (2018, p. 294) argues, such emphasis on the need to restore national sovereignty and re-territorialize state power, that is what we earlier defined as sovereignism, is what actually bonds together all populist movements, across the range from left to right, regardless of their inclusive or exclusive nature.

Quite surprisingly, although the concept of sovereignism appears to be key in populist discourse, it has been taken for granted and under-theorized by scholars dealing with populism. For instance, in the introduction to *The Oxford Handbook of Populism*, Rovira Kaltwasser et al. (2017, p. 2) argue that

> the origin of the term can be traced further back in time through the modern history of democratic legitimacy … In the history of modern democracy 'the people' emerge not only as the source of political authority, but also as unified entity able to act and to retrieve power from government officials: the *sovereign people*. This popular ground legitimizes democratic politics but also paves the way for populism. (see also Kelly, 2017)

5. A new research agenda

In order to fill the gap, it would be useful to focus on the linkage between populism and sovereignism, and to propose a new research agenda with which to study populist mobilization and the current challenges to representative democracy and supranational integration. Indeed, although the theoretical insights introduced in the previous section offer some relevant ideas for better grasping this linkage, there are other crucial issues that remain to be addressed:

5.1. Sovereignism as an aspect of populist discourse, but not exclusive to it

Although appeals to national sovereignty can be detected in several parties, not necessarily qualified as populist, they can be considered some of the recurrent and core themes of populist discourse. Indeed, sovereignist claims pre-exist populism, but populism simply took over ideas such as those of popular sovereignty and of the regaining of decision-making power under a narrower, territorial authority, which coincides with the national state. In other words, while sovereignism might exist without populism, there is no populist discourse that does not include sovereignist claims. This argument, however, poses the crucial question of the need to clearly identify what differentiates the sovereignty claims of mainstream parties from those waved by populist actors. In other words, how can we distinguish between the claims of the UK Conservative Prime Minister, Theresa May, to 'restore national self-determination' and UKIP leader Nigel Farage's similar pleas for the UK's 'right of self-determination'? As the following points also seem to suggest, a possible, initial answer to such a crucial question is that populism merely re-elaborates on sovereignist claims, by emphasizing the blame placed on the establishment and the mechanisms of representative democracy as being chiefly responsible for the uncertainties and unresponsiveness of the current democratic systems.

5.2. Sovereignism as a distinct concept

While some might argue that sovereignism is just 'old wine in new bottles', we contend that it is distinct from other concepts. For instance, sovereignism shares with nationalism the promotion of the nation, its superiority, self-determination, and exclusive right to decide. However, as argued earlier, sovereignism is a form of grievance, a reaction that aims at bringing back control within a specific territory, namely the nation state. It emphasizes the need to *restore* authority to the place where it was supposedly originally conceived and the *reaction against the shifts of authority away* from the national boundaries. This concept therefore explicitly aims at restoring the state's sovereignty, that is the absolute or exclusive capacity of decision-making within a specific territory and, more generally, the 'ability to determine ... [the nation's] own destiny and care of the welfare of its citizens' (Grimm, 2015, p. ix). The restoration of the past does not necessarily mean, however, that this past really existed. According to Freeden, for populism, and right-wing populism in particular, sovereignty is seen

> not merely as the spatial control over territory but the appropriation of a temporal trajectory of 'we were here first', hence we are the ultimate deciders, the *fons et origo* of what matters and happens here, and hence also we always have precedence over immigrants, disregarding the fact that our ancestors were immigrants too. (Freeden, 2017, p. 4)

The focus on restoration, on the recovery of a (real or imaginary) past explains why sovereignism has a peculiar meaning, and cannot be considered as a proxy of a nationalist claim, although the two are closely related and might sometimes overlap. Moreover, while nationalism also embraces cultural and socio-psychological aspects, sovereignism focuses specifically on the aspect of (restored) 'control' over a defined territory (Ichijo, 2009, p. 159; Sheehan, 2006). Likewise, sovereignism has strong ties to Euroscepticism (Leconte, 2010; Szczerbiak & Taggart, 2007), especially as a claim for national sovereignty. However, sovereignism explicitly puts forward an alternative proposal for the distribution of authority, and clearly redefines the polity within national boundaries, while Euroscepticism does not necessarily include such specific counter-proposals. Furthermore, Euroscepticism should not necessarily be considered as a sharp rejection of supranational integration; rather, it should be conceived as an attitude ranging from 'soft' criticism of the current shape of the European project, and thus claims for its reform, to 'hard', principled opposition to the European Union, invoking the return to the previous system of independent, European nation-states (Szczerbiak & Taggart, 2007). Nonetheless, if sovereignism is to be considered as crucial for the understanding of populism, further research is required to clarify any likely overlap with other concepts.

5.3. Sovereignism as a multidimensional concept

Sovereignism can be conceived as a multi-faceted response to socio-economic, cultural and political challenges. It might therefore assume different forms and refer to different scopes of action, including: popular (or political) sovereignism, that is the idea that 'the will of the people is considered the ultimate source of legitimacy' (Spruyt, Keppens, & Van Droogenbroeck, 2016, p. 336), as opposed to parliamentary sovereignism (Wellings & Vines, 2016); national sovereignism, as opposed to the supranational sovereignism embodied, for example, by the European Union; and economic sovereignism, as a claim for a political economy that could be beneficial for the (national) people's wealth. If sovereignist claims are the core themes of the populist discourse, the multidimensionality of the concept of sovereignism then explains the intrinsic ideological heterogeneity of populist parties; at the same time, it strengthens the argument that references to 'taking back the control', although articulated according to different spheres of sovereignty, are what actually bonds together otherwise different parties. Moreover, parties might combine more than one dimension in a geometry-variable perspective. For instance, the Spanish, leftist Podemos claims to restore the control of political and economic sovereignty back to the national level, but it is utterly distant from the emphasis on border control that features within the right-wing and exclusive Dutch Party for Freedom (PVV), or the Italian Lega. Nonetheless, as Kallis (2018, p. 298) argues, while focusing on different dimensions of sovereignty, 'the two projects converge on the reinvention of the border – symbolic and physical – of the existing nation states as the marker of redeemed sovereignty'. Hence, by unfolding the multidimensionality of sovereignism, it would be possible to have a better understanding of the complexity of the populist phenomenon, while at the same time avoiding the trap of its tendency to 'escape generalisation'.

5.4. Sovereignism as an anti-establishment discourse

A crucial dimension of sovereignism is, as seen above, that of popular (or political) sovereignty. It could be defined as the appeal to give control back to ordinary citizens, who perceive the institutions and elites of such a 'diffuse' and 'dispersed' form of sovereignty as distant, unresponsive, ineffective and disrespectful of the real interest of the people. This implies a broader challenge towards the establishment:

> In a populist democracy the political domain consequently extends into spheres not considered 'political' in a liberal democracy: media, judiciary, culture, the economy and education are allegedly no longer largely impartial and non-political institutions, but all spheres which are political and over which 'the people' consequently should be able to exert influence. (Corduwener, 2014, p. 432)

Elites are thus described as actors that undermine 'true' sovereignty and consequently incapable of defending ordinary citizens from the threats to their culture, identity, economic wealth, and security. Likewise, the national elites who built supranational institutions are perceived as mainly responsible for the legal framework, or the lack thereof, of the global economic system. To this purpose, Kallis (2018, p. 296) offers an interesting insight: what qualifies the populist reframing of sovereignist arguments is the emphasis on the 'panegyric redemption of sovereignty from the grip of the internationalized/globalized agents that needs to be performed'.

This is actually even in line with the scholarly arguments suggesting that the European Union was built with the 'permissive consensus' of the mainstream parties, with limited forms of political opposition, especially at its onset (Hooghe & Marks, 2009). Accordingly, new research agenda should therefore examine the populist anti-establishment rhetoric as a reframing of sovereignist arguments, and clearly spell out when sovereignist appeals to popular sovereignty become populist anti-establishment claims. The following examples, albeit with some oversimplification, would better explain the populist re-elaboration of sovereignist arguments. For instance, a typical identitarian sovereignist argument promotes the restoration of the national control of borders in order to prevent migration flows; in its populist re-elaboration, the lost control of national borders is the result of an elite-driven project, put forward regardless of citizens' consent, that has made such borders porous and blurred, while promoting ineffective forms of transnational cooperation. Likewise, economic sovereignism claims to regain the state's full sovereignty over economic decision-making; however, according to the populists' reframing, by endorsing the integration of markets, the globalized elites and the national mainstream parties have weakened the authority of the state and its capacity to protect the (national) people's wealth and well-being; moreover, the elites are accused of having pursued these processes without the consent of the (mostly unaware) represented people. Finally, the transformation of sovereignty has implied a shift of the centres of authority away from nation-states, thus triggering the political sovereignist demands to bring institutions back within the national borders. Populists reformulated these claims by blaming the distant, unaccountable, and unresponsive elites of cutting citizens off from decision-making, whose dynamics are increasingly perceived as opaque.

5.5. Sovereignism as criticism of representative democracy

Sovereignist claims mainly target representative democracy, which has been established as the prevailing model of the nation-state – flourishing during the process of democratization, and challenged by globalization. Indeed, it has favoured the processes of globalization, but has ended up being deeply transformed by it. As previously argued, liberal democracy has increasingly been perceived as falling short of adequately addressing the challenges posed by the transformations of sovereignty and has therefore been blamed as a main source of insecurity by sovereignist claims. Likewise, the ideological core of populism is nourished by what Urbinati (2019) defines as the *demos*, namely the people, and the emphasis on the need to retrieve power from politicians, which closely relates to populists' ambivalence about representative democracy. The 'people' that populist actors usually refer to is a homogeneous, though vaguely undefined entity who are unheard by politicians, and whose 'purity' is threatened by the procedures of mediation and compromise that traditionally feature in representative democracy (Mastropaolo, 2017). As a consequence, the populist discourse promotes alternative forms of representation and decision-making, which are likely to overcome the power of the established elites and their institutions. In particular, populist movements make a claim for more direct democracy, which would confer power to people. Populism thus promotes a form of government power, alternative to representative democracy, based on a large, unmediated, non-institutionalized support for the personalistic leader, defined by Urbinati (2019, p. 9) as 'direct representation'. In populists' ideal world, representative democracy would be better replaced by a system in which mechanisms of direct democracy combine with the power of the leader, with a reduced role for any form of intermediaries between the people and the decision-makers (that is to say, the parties). Against this backdrop, the new research agenda on populism and sovereignism should therefore further explore how the populist ambivalence, if not rejection of representative democracy actually relates to the sovereignist blame placed on this democratic model.

5.6. Sovereignism as citizens' and political actors' claims

Sovereignism might be seen and analyzed from both a supply-side and demand-side perspective. From a supply-side perspective, sovereignism, and its populist re-elaboration, is an actor-driven discourse, denouncing the elite for hindering people's sovereignty, with the (bad) elites/political representatives portrayed as those who have 'sold out' people's sovereignty to supranational powers and/or outsiders (such as immigrants). It also includes a promise of change in order to restore people's sovereignty, a change that would be ensured only by trusting the 'new' leaders and their parties. Upon these premises, a research agenda that links populism and sovereignism should investigate whether populist parties play the role of 'entrepreneurs' of sovereignist claims, and to what extent these claims exert a contagion towards the mainstream parties. In a demand-side perspective, sovereignism might be seen as a latent or explicit demand in favour of national independence, re-bordering orientations and direct democracy, and against crisis and uncertainty, the establishment and representative democracy and supranational power (much like a Eurosceptic sentiment). This makes compelling further analyses on the relevance of claims in citizens' attitudes and how this relates to party preferences for populist actors.

6. Research contributions for the new research agenda: a special issue

The suggested research agenda mainly aims at 'sowing doubts, rather than gathering certainties' (Bobbio, 2005). The six research issues outlined above should actually be considered as open-ended questions, still in need of further theoretical and empirical inputs, rather than 'yardsticks' for the sovereignism-populism linkage.

The complexity of this research agenda is also reflected in the five articles included in this Special Issue focusing on populism and sovereignty. They all explore, in different, yet complementary ways, specific aspects of this multifaceted relationship. By using a wide-range of methodological approaches, these articles include sovereignism and populism either as dependent or independent variables and thus provide an encompassing analysis of the two phenomena, their linkage, and the main theoretical and substantial implications of such a relationship. As for the research design, most contributions offer a fine-grained analysis, through a case-study research design, while the comparative study by Basile, Borri and Verzichelli (2020) explores the sovereignist-populist linkage by using European-wide data. Furthermore, some of the articles focus on the 'supply' side of sovereignism and populism (Baldini, Bressanelli, & Gianfreda 2020; Ivaldi & Mazzoleni 2020), thus investigating the nature of the sovereignist discourse in political parties; on the other hand, Basile, Borri, & Verzichelli (2020) and Mueller and Heidelberger (2020) focus on the 'demand' side, by examining, respectively, the determinants of the support for sovereignist claims, and the impact of the support for such claims on voting choices. Finally, Heinisch, Werner and Habersack (2020) focus on both the 'demand' and the 'supply' side, by examining party discourses as well as voting preferences for sovereignist and populist parties in the Austrian case.

Although conceived as standalone papers on the topic in question, these contributions overall address the aforementioned six research lines from different perspectives and approaches, providing valuable insights to the theoretical and empirical debate. In particular, by proposing compound, though diverse operationalizations of the concept, all the articles seem to point to the need to conceive of sovereignism as an intrinsically multidimensional concept. Interestingly, the tension between sovereignism and populism emerges in these five studies, which engage in a critical and insightful effort to propose theoretical and empirical grounds to the debated demarcation line between populism and sovereignism, and the nature of their linkage.

Yet beyond the theoretical and empirical contribution to literature, and besides their interest from a scholarly point of view, the findings of these articles also carry substantial implications. By unravelling the context in which sovereignist claims originate, they indicate the main sources of the increasing popularity of sovereignist claims, as well as at least some of the reasons for their growing appeal among the European electorates. They reveal common patterns across different European countries, thus drawing attention to the likely consequences of sovereignist and populist phenomena on the eve of the European elections of 2019. Indeed, contrary to what was argued at the beginning of this section, among the many 'doubts' that it triggers, a certainty is likely to emerge from this scholarly effort: Sovereignism is increasingly relevant in the contemporary political discourse, and it is ultimately likely to develop as a distinct cleavage of political competition. Coupled with their growing electoral success, the great capacity of populist actors to feed on sovereignist claims inevitably poses a challenge to the projects of supranational integration, and at the same time, urges a timely rethinking of democratic politics in a context of increasing globalization and regionalization, as already suggested long ago by Held and McGrew (1995). Indeed, the guardians of representative democracy should clearly spell out, and put forward, far-sighted alternatives to 'taking back control', before sovereignist fences and walls are built as a shield to contemporary challenges.

ORCID

Linda Basile ⓘ http://orcid.org/0000-0003-2842-1264
Oscar Mazzoleni ⓘ http://orcid.org/0000-0002-2535-613X

References

Agnew, J. (2009). *Globalization and sovereignty*. Lanham, MD: Rowman & Littlefield Publishers.

Akkerman, A., Mudde, C., & Zaslove, A. (2014). How populist are the people? Measuring populist attitudes in voters. *Comparative Political Studies*, *47*(9), 1324–1353.

Albertazzi, D., Giovannini, A., & Seddone, A. (2018). 'No regionalism please, we are *Leghisti*!' The transformation of the Italian Lega Nord under the leadership of Matteo Salvini. *Regional & Federal Studies*, *28*(5), 645–671.

Aschauer, W. (2017). Societal malaise in turbulent times: Introducing a new explanatory factor for populism from a cross-national Europe-wide perspective. In R. Heinisch, C. Holtz-Bacha, & O. Mazzoleni (Eds.), *Political populism. A handbook* (pp. 307–328). Baden-Baden: Nomos.

Attinà, F. (2016). Migration drivers, the EU external migration policy and crisis management. *Romanian Journal of European Affairs*, *16*(4), 15–31.

Baldini, G, Bressanelli, E, & Gianfreda, S. (2020). Taking Back Control? Brexit, Sovereignism and Populism in Westminster (2015-17). *European Politics and Society*, *21*(2), 219–234.

Basile, L., Borri, R, & Verzichelli, L. (2020). For Whom the Sovereignist Bell Tolls?" Individual determinants of support for sovereignism in ten European countries. *European Politics and Society*, *21*(2), 235–257.

Bobbio, N. (2005). *Politica e cultura*. (F. Sbarberi, Ed.). Torino: Einaudi.

Clarke, H., Goodwin, M., & Whiteley, P. (2017). *Brexit: Why Britain voted to leave the European Union*. Cambridge: Cambridge University Press.

Corduwener, P. (2014). The populist conception of democracy beyond popular sovereignty. *Journal of Contemporary European Research*, *10*(4), 423–437.

Dahlberg, S., & Linde, J. (2016). Losing happily? The mitigating effect of democracy and quality of government on the winner-loser gap in political support. *International Journal of Public Administration*, *39*(9), 652–664.

De Cleen, B. (2017). Populism and nationalism. In R. Kaltwasser, C. Taggart, P. Ostiguy, & P. Ochoa Espejo (Eds.), *The Oxford handbook of populism* (pp. 342–362). Oxford: Oxford University Press.

De Cleen, B., & Stavrakakis, Y. (2017). Distinctions and articulations: A discourse theoretical framework for the study of populism and nationalism. *Javnost – The Public*, *24*(4), 301–319.

de la Torre, C. (2019). *Routledge handbook of global populism*. London: Routledge.

De Spiegeleire, S., Skinner, C., Sweijs, T., Mendonça Oliveira, M., Siebenga, R., Bekkers, F., & Farnham, N. (2017). *The rise of populist sovereignism: What it is, where it comes from, and what it means for international security and defense*. The Hague: Hague Centre for Strategic Studies.

Freeden, M. (2017). After the Brexit referendum: revisiting populism as an ideology. *Journal of Political Ideologies*, *22*, 1–11.

Grimm, D. (2015). *Sovereignty. The origin and the future of a political and legal concept*. New York: University of Columbia Press.

Heinisch, R, Holtz-Bacha, C, & Mazzoleni, O. (2017). *Political Populism. A Handbook*. Baden-Baden: Nomos.

Heinisch, R, Werner, A, & Habersack, F. (2020). Reclaiming National Sovereignty: The Case of the Conservatives and the Far Right in Austria. *European Politics and Society*, *21*(2), 163–181.

Held, D. (1995). *Democracy and the global order: From the modern state to cosmopolitan governance*. Cambridge: Polity Press.

Held, D., & McGrew, A. (1993). Globalization and the liberal democratic state. *Government and Opposition*, *28*(3), 361–371.

Hooghe, L., & Marks, G. (2003). Unraveling the central state, but how? Types of multi-level governance. *American Political Science Review*, *97*(2), 233–243.

Hooghe, L., & Marks, G. (2009). A postfunctionalist theory of European integration: From permissive-consensus to constraining dissensus. *British Journal of Political Science*, *39*(1), 1–23.

Ichijo, A. (2009). Sovereignty and nationalism in the twenty-first century: The Scottish case. *Ethnopolitics*, *8*(2), 155–172.

Ivaldi, G, & Mazzoleni, O. (2020). Economic Populism and Sovereigntism: The Economic Supply of European Radical Right-Wing Populist Parties. *European Politics and Society*, *21*(2), 202–218.

Kallis, A. (2018). Populism, sovereigntism, and the unlikely re-emergence of the territorial nation-state. *Fudan Journal of the Humanities and Social Sciences, 11*(3), 285–302.

Keating, M. (2003). Sovereignty and plurinational democracy: Problems in political science. In N. Walker (Ed.), *Sovereignty in transition* (pp. 191–208). Oxford: Hart Publishing.

Kelly, D. (2017). Populism and the history of popular sovereignty. In R. Kaltwasser, C. Taggart, P. Ostiguy, & P. Ochoa Espejo (Eds.), *The Oxford handbook of populism* (pp. 511–534). Oxford: Oxford University Press.

Kriesi, H., Grande, E., Dolezal, M., Helbling, M., Höglinger, D., Hutter, S., & Wüest, B. (2012). *Political conflict in Western Europe*. Cambridge: Cambridge University Press.

Leconte, C. (2010). *Understanding Euroscepticism*. London: Red Globe Press.

Lord, C., & Beetham, D. (2001). Legitimizing the EU: Is there a 'post-parliamentary basis' for its legitimation? *Journal of Common Market Studies, 39*(3), 443–462.

Mann, M. (1997). Has globalization ended the rise and rise of the nation-state? *Review of International Political Economy, 4*(3), 472–496.

Mastropaolo, A. (2017). Populism and political representation. In R. Heinisch, C. Holtz-Bacha, & O. Mazzoleni (Eds.), *Political populism. A handbook* (pp. 59–72). Baden Baden: Nomos.

Mazzoleni, O., & Ruzza, C. (2018). Combining regionalism and nationalism: The Lega in Italy and the Lega dei Ticinesi in Switzerland. *Comparative European Politics, 16*(6), 976–992.

Mudde, C. (2007). *Populist radical right parties in Europe*. Cambridge: Cambridge University Press.

Papadopoulos, Y. (2010). Accountability and multi-level governance: More accountability, less democracy? *West European Politics, 33*(5), 1030–1049.

Rovira Kaltwasser, C., Taggart, P., & Ostiguy, P. (2017). Populism. An overview of the concept and the state of the art. In P. Ochoa Espejo, C. Rovira Kaltwasser, P. Taggart, P. Ostiguy, & P. Ochoa Espejo (Eds.), *The Oxford handbook of populism* (pp. 1–24). Oxford: Oxford University Press.

Sassen, S. (1996). *Losing control? Sovereignty in the age of globalization*. New York: Columbia University Press.

Sassen, S. (2008). *Territory, authority, rights. From medieval to global assemblages*. Princeton: Princeton University Press.

Scharpf, F. (1999). *Governing in Europe: Effective and democratic?* Oxford: Oxford University Press.

Sheehan, J. J. (2006). Presidential address: The problem of sovereignty in European history. *The American Historical Review, 111*(1), 1–15.

Smith, D. A., Solinger, D. J., & Topik, S. C. (1999). *State and sovereignty in the global economy*. London: Routledge.

Spruyt, B., Keppens, G., & Van Droogenbroeck, F. (2016). *Who* supports populism and *what* attracts people to it? *Political Research Quarterly, 69*(2), 335–346.

Strange, S. (1996). *The retreat of the state. The diffusion of power in the world economy*. Cambridge: Cambridge University Press.

Szczerbiak, A., & Taggart, P. (2007). Introduction: Opposing Europe? The politics of Euroscepticism in Europe. In A. Szczerbiak & P. Taggart (Eds.), *Opposing Europe? The comparative party politics of Euroscepticism* (pp. 1–15). Oxford: Oxford University Press.

Urbinati, N. (2019). Political theory of populism. *Annual Review of Political Science, 22*(1), 111–127.

Van Creveld, M. (1999). *The rise and decline of the state*. Cambridge: Cambridge University Press.

Wellings, B., & Vines, E. (2016). Populism and sovereignty: The EU Act and the in-out referendum, 2010–2015. *Parliamentary Affairs, 69*(2), 309–326.

ᵭ OPEN ACCESS

Reclaiming national sovereignty: the case of the conservatives and the far right in Austria

Reinhard Heinisch ⓘ, Annika Werner ⓘ and Fabian Habersack ⓘ

ABSTRACT
This article investigates how and why Austrian parties have (re)constructed claims of national sovereignty and brought them to the centre of political competition. Theoretically, claims for national sovereignty are directed at recovering the people's autonomy from 'sinister' elites and 'harmful' outsiders like immigrants. As such claims vary in terms of policy content, salience, and discursive means, this article uses the analysis of manifestos and speeches to ascertain how the radical-right populist Austrian Freedom Party (FPÖ) constructed sovereignty claims in 2013 and 2017. Furthermore, it shows how the mainstream right Austrian People's Party (ÖVP) adopted these claims, significantly narrowing the gap to the far-right FPÖ on the national and economic dimension of sovereignty, and largely renounced its pro-European and anti-sovereignist positions by 2017. In a second step, we examine whether the claims by these two parties match the preferences of their voters. Here, the findings suggest that the FPÖ's sovereignty claims broadly correspond to the demands of its voters whereas ÖVP voters only partially express support for such claims, mainly on the national sovereignty investigating in detail the form and conditions of their occurrence.

Introduction

After decades of globalization and denationalization (Kriesi et al., 2006), radical-right and, as of recently, centre-right parties across Western Europe are rediscovering and reclaiming the values of sovereignty (Hainsworth, 2016; Meguid, 2005; 2010; Meijers, 2017; Pytlas, 2015). For European democracies, the latter part of the twentieth century was defined by deepening integration so that differences between nations and their borders seemed to disappear, giving way to new, supranational governance mechanisms and transnational identities. However, in the wake of multiple crises, political actors across European party systems have responded to the new socio-political circumstances by calling for the reassertion of greater national control over internationally shared policy

---

This is an Open Access article distributed under the terms of the Creative Commons Attribution-NonCommercial-NoDerivatives License (http://creativecommons.org/licenses/by-nc-nd/4.0/), which permits non-commercial re-use, distribution, and reproduction in any medium, provided the original work is properly cited, and is not altered, transformed, or built upon in any way.

areas. They have also advocated 'handing back the power to the people', suggesting (inter-)national elites had for too long served only their own agenda. Being an integrated part of an increasingly globalized world, Austria has not been exempted from these developments.

Our research is motivated by recent changes in Austrian party politics that have particularly affected the Christian-conservative Austrian People's Party (ÖVP) and the radical-right populist Freedom Party (FPÖ). Stuck in third place among Austria's major parties for most of the time in the period between 2013 and 2017, the ÖVP went through a rapid succession of different party leaders culminating in the ascendance of the young Sebastian Kurz to the leadership post shortly before the 2017 national election. Although the FPÖ had led the opinion polls for most of the time prior to 2017, it had remained politically isolated. As a result, it increasingly signalled its willingness to moderate its positions somewhat (Akkerman, de Lange, & Rooduijn, 2015) in order to join a coalition with one of the mainstream parties with which its agenda was sufficiently compatible. Whereas the ÖVP had traditionally been the country's staunchest advocate of European integration, even calling itself *Europapartei* (party of Europe), the FPÖ had long been a champion of 'taking back control'. Recently, these calls for national autonomy and their underlying arguments have been taken up by the mainstream right under Kurz. He has since led his party to victory in the 2017 elections and assumed the position of chancellor in a coalition with the FPÖ.

Using data derived from party manifestos and party leader speeches, this article analyses how Austrian parties on the political right have constructed calls for 'renationalization'. The ÖVP appears to be moving from the pro-integration position to a stance that is increasingly sceptical of internationalization. As this development is neither uniform nor clear-cut, it is not yet well understood. Thus, this article examines – in light of the Austrian case – how radical-right populist and right-wing mainstream parties construct sovereignist claims, the extent to which these claims are similar, and whether or not they develop in similar ways. This entails first disentangling claims towards national, popular, and economic sovereignty (Basile & Mazzoleni, 2019, pp. 6–7). Second, we analyse which policy areas are most often seen as a priority for reasserting sovereignty. Against this backdrop, finally, we investigate how such appeals to sovereignty are connected with voter demand and whether demand-side explanations, might therefore drive party change.

The right reclaims national, economic, and popular sovereignty

Over the past decade, party positions along with voters' attitudes have clearly shifted to the right in the context of Europe's multiple crises (Krzyżanowski, 2017; Luo, 2017). The seeming inability of political institutions to anticipate and prevent the economic and financial crises of 2008, and the related Eurozone debt crisis that began in 2010, undermined trust in mainstream political elites and European institutions. Nationally unpopular policy decisions by supranational institutions, such as the imposition of sanctions on Russia, have fuelled this anger and mistrust. Radical-right populist and conservative parties across Europe were well positioned to pick up on these sentiments. Whereas the former benefitted from their history of Euroscepticism and anti-globalization rhetoric, the conservatives could point to their association with cultural traditionalism and regionalism.

Populism may be understood as an ideological construct or claim (present in a discourse or set of attitudes) postulating an antagonism between the 'people' and the 'others' in a Manichean manner. As such, the sovereignty of the people is the essential element of the populist discourse. As Basile and Mazzoleni (in the introduction of this issue) argue in this issue, sovereignism, conceived as the need to restore national sovereignty and re-territorialise state power, bonds together all populist movements. By emphasizing internal and external threats to sovereignty, sovereignism often becomes a self-proclaimed *raison d'être* of populist actors. Nonetheless, right-wing populists share concerns about sovereignty with conservatives and other parties of the right. Thus, calls for sovereignism are expected to closely resemble different aspects of both radical-right and populist positions, as sovereignism shares nativism with the former and people-centredness and elite-scepticism with the latter. Theory would lead us to surmise, however, that there are distinctive aspects about sovereignty that pertain primarily to populism as will be shown below.

For the case of the Austrian political system, this raises several questions: First, how have the radical-right populist FPÖ and the conservative ÖVP constructed such claims about the need to regain popular, national, and/or economic sovereignty? Second, which policy areas have been primarily targeted in conjunction with this strategy? Third, are there differences between the radical-right populist Freedom Party and the conservative People's Party? Here the issue is to what extent the ÖVP has adopted the populist aspects of sovereignty claims. And finally, it also raises the question of the extent to which developments on the supply side are rooted in the preferences of those who vote for either the ÖVP or the FPÖ. In the Austrian political system, the FPÖ has for a long time been the only potential representative of voters with sovereignist positions. In general, the dominant party and representation literature assumes that parties seek to win elections and thus take up positions that are favourable amongst their supporters (Downs, 1957).

Knowing that populism is not just a supply-side phenomenon, but is also shaped by the demand side, we shed light on voters' preferences and changes from 2013 to 2017. We make the theoretical assumptions that the sovereignty preferences expressed by populist and conservative parties are matched by their voters. Thus, we would expect to see populist evidence of a preference for popular sovereignty with FPÖ voters, whereas conservative party voters show the least support for economic protectionism (economic sovereignty), but relatively the most for national sovereignty.

National, economic, and popular sovereignty and their causes

In our first research question, we turn to the target of sovereignist claims. The assertion of sovereignist values intersects with a broad range of policy areas but depends on the particular goals a political actor hopes to achieve. It is the latter that shapes the framing of such messages. In keeping with the conceptual outline of the special issue, we focus explicitly on three equally important variants of sovereignism: national, economic, and popular sovereignism. The former seeks to defend national borders against external rather than internal 'threats'. Its narrative is based on an alleged dichotomy between the nation's 'own people' and the cultural 'others', describing how rapidly worsening conditions and growing polarization between the two antagonistic groups and between the national people and supranational elites and institutions require a radical change of direction as a matter of national urgency.

While national sovereignism focuses on the defence of the 'good people' against the cultural other, economic sovereignism refers to the idea that economic policies should be primarily beneficial for the 'own' people's wealth. Triggered by the loss of national control over economic developments due to globalization, as was highlighted by the global financial crisis, claims for economic sovereignty address the perceived threat to the jobs and welfare of the national people. Rejection of international trade agreements, 'bringing jobs back' from other countries, and closing the national labour market to non-national workers are examples for such claims. In making such policy proposals, populists seek to capitalize on the sentiments of working class voters and those feeling economically disadvantaged (Betz & Meret, 2012; Brubaker, 2017; Moffitt, 2016).

The third variant, popular sovereignism, is a closely related narrative. It first refers to claims that the sovereign 'people' are the only source for legitimating political power and authority (Spruyt, Keppens, & van Droogenbroeck, 2016, p. 336) and implies that supranational bodies represent unaccountable elites whose interests are divorced from those of the 'true people'. This populist argument extends to the domestic arena and, for instance, stands in conflict with parliamentarism by alleging that contemporary political systems are dominated by 'corrupt political elites' working against the interests of the 'good people'. Popular sovereignism and other variants such as national sovereignism may appear together, so that opposition to the EU may be motivated by charges of a 'democratic deficit' in decision-making and/or by fears of being controlled by 'foreign' interests. Likewise, the references to permeable borders and the influx of migrants tap into the same national sovereignist logic alleging that far-away political elites do not care about or are wilfully complicit in these developments. Against this, popular sovereignist claims put forth the idea of 'handing back the power to the people' through direct democratic tools.

Of the three types of sovereignty, we would expect the populists – in this case the FPÖ – to put the greatest emphasis on popular sovereignty, when compared to their conservative competitors. Moreover, Taggart writing about Populism's 'empty heart' (2000, p. 4) and Kitschelt (1995) discussing populism's winning formulas both suggest that populists are especially skilled in advancing ambivalent and contradictory positions. Thus, claims combining leftist objectives such as economic protectionism with far-right ideas such as nationalism should be expected in the case of the FPÖ. By contrast, we would assume a conservative pro-business party like the ÖVP (or its electorate) to share many of the FPÖ's positions on national sovereignty, but be more moderate on economic and popular sovereignty.

Which policy fields are targeted in constructing national, economic, and popular sovereignty – and how?

Turning now to specific policy positions, we wonder which issue areas are at the centre of sovereignist claims and how they connect to the national, economic, and popular sovereignty dimensions. As populism is a 'thin ideology' (Stanley, 2008), it does not prescribe specific policy positions. However, the stronger focus of the three dimensions of sovereignism on specific societal outcomes allows for a more targeted discussion. Unsurprisingly, policies and politics related to the European Union have been a central theme in the remake of sovereignist claims. In Austria and elsewhere, conservatives found themselves at a crossroads between remaining pro-Europeans or – as has been observable during the last decade – adopting a more ambivalent posture (Kriesi et al., 2006; Krzyżanowski, 2017). Meijers (2017) speaks of 'contagious Euroscepticism' in reference to conservatives shifting their EU policy closer to the discourse practiced by the far right. For the construction of sovereignist claims in Austria, this means that EU issues are selectively employed by pointing to the benefit of EU membership whenever it is expedient. This may take the form of supporting economic integration and even military cooperation to secure EU borders while simultaneously rejecting EU institutions as 'enemies' wilfully working against Austrian interests. For our analysis, it will be particularly interesting to see to what degree this equivocal Euroscepticism (Heinisch, McDonnell, & Werner, 2018) plays out in parties' manifestos and leader speeches, as well as which particular areas serve as the basis for giving EU policy a sovereignist 'Austria first' spin.

The reassertion of sovereignty is by no means limited to criticism of European integration. Claims of economic sovereignism will likely also find expression in the rejection of international and multilateral trade agreements and hostility to all that supposedly threatens national economic autonomy. Nonetheless, this presents parties on the mainstream right with a strategic dilemma since 'economically they tend to endorse liberalization, but socially and culturally they tend to be nationalists and opposed to the opening up of borders' (Kriesi et al., 2006, p. 927). Thus, capitalizing on nationalist economic messages holds greater appeal.

With regard to national sovereignism, immigration policy has been one of the most prominent areas for re-asserting such claims (Krzyżanowski, 2017). This allows parties to mobilize on fears of security risks and also provides an expedient response to salient issues such as the refugee crises. Positions favouring greater border security and more restrictive immigration policies alongside strict 'law and order' positions are directly connected with calls to [preserve] 'one's own culture' against what is deemed 'foreign' and 'harmful' (Bale, 2008). As these two policy areas provide clear opportunities for re-asserting national-sovereignist values *and* have become especially salient, we would expect centre-right and far-right parties to develop pronounced and clear postures on these issues.

Related to immigration and integration policies are social policies where the central claim is about taking action against 'welfare abuse' and regulating labour market mobility for the benefit of one's 'own people' (Bale, 2010). Schumacher and van Kersbergen (2014) suggest that such claims serve a 'back to the nation-state' function which is also central to the politics of identity, culture and religion (Hafez, 2014). Analytically, we would therefore expect to find both the centre right and far right to emphasize identity politics equally strongly and present the 'risk of Islam' as a serious threat to national sovereignty.

Finally, as calls for popular sovereignty are focused on procedural aspects of transferring decision-making capacity from the elites directly to the people, these could be connected to any policy field. Based on the definition of popular sovereignty, such claims are most likely calling for the renationalization of decision-making competences, or for the introduction of direct democratic instruments for any salient policy issue.

The Austrian party system and the construction of sovereignty

Before turning to the empirical part, we need to introduce the Austrian case and the two political parties at the centre of the analysis. Since entering the European Union in 1995,

Austria has experienced a growing salience of cultural and immigration issues, compared to economic questions resulting in voter sentiments of deprivation from self-determination (Dolezal, 2008; Kriesi et al., 2006). Against this backdrop, rediscovering and reframing sovereignist values has played a major role, making the country a crucial case for the analysis of parties and candidates operating with such appeals.

In the context of post-war economic growth and modernization resulting in the disappearance of traditional political milieus, Christian democratic and conservative parties moved to the centre, as new middle and professional classes became willing constituents who supported a more liberal and internationalist policy orientation (Heinisch, 2002). Pursuing a staunchly pro-European agenda, centre-conservative parties could also distinguish themselves politically from the centre left that had for a long time been more sceptical of the promises of market integration and economic authority transfer to the supranational level. This was especially the case in Austria where the ÖVP took the lead in the early 1980s in reorienting the country's SPÖ-led global foreign policy orientation of the previous decade to an almost exclusively Europe-centred strategy (Heinisch, 2002; Luif, 1995). As Social Democratic parties followed suit and also became champions of European integration and liberal internationalism, which was the case in Austria from the mid-1980s onward, only the radical-right populists and the left remained opposed to this direction. When the Austrian Greens changed their position on the country's EU membership in the wake of overwhelming support for Austria's accession to the EU in a referendum in 1994, the FPÖ became the only party in parliament to offer a political home to Eurosceptical voters.

Examining sovereigntist appeals in Austrian party competition requires a systematic mapping of how such claims unfold and whether they match with the preferences of these parties. Thus, the central question of our analysis is how this is achieved (which policy areas are addressed for what goals) and in what way these claims are presented (i.e. content, direction and scope). Subsequently, we turn to the voters of the two parties to ascertain where and to what extent there is demand for the policy shifts we observe. This analysis rests on the crucial assumption that parties are at least partially vote-seeking and thus reactive to the shifts in their voters' opinions (e.g. Downs, 1957).

Methods: measuring claims of national, economic, and popular sovereignty

How do the FPÖ and ÖVP construct their claims of national sovereignty and *in which policy areas* does this agenda become visible? To answer these questions, we conduct a text analysis of (a) the two parties' election manifestos in 2013 and 2017 as the primary and condensed outlet for the party programmes, and (b) of parliamentary speeches by the party leaders from 2013 to the end of 2017, which provide more room for nuance and argumentation. The speeches analysed are those of party leaders and the respective heads of the party's parliamentary faction – the two most important national-level representatives of each party. These were Heinz-Christian Strache (party leader) and Herbert Kickl (head of faction) for the FPÖ, and Michael Spindelegger, Reinhold Mitterlehner, and Sebastian Kurz (party leaders within this period) and Reinhold Lopakta (head of faction) for the ÖVP.

The content analysis for both manifesto and speeches consists of three steps. First, we identify all claims regarding sovereignty. In accordance with the conceptual frameworks, these text fragments are then categorized into national, economic, and popular claims. Furthermore, we identified statements making claims *against* Austrian sovereignty, such as those expressing preferences for transferring new powers from the national to the supranational level. The main analysis is based on the four manifestos, allowing for a systematic and comparative investigation of how the two parties construct sovereignty and whether any changes occurred from 2013 to 2017. The speeches provide important additional information for contextualizing seemingly contradictory or vague claims.

We define 'asserting national sovereignty and autonomy' as all those claims seeking to defend or maintain national authority over certain values and policy areas. The resulting claims usually range from one to three sentences. The second analytical step encompassed the categorization of the claims into national, economic, and popular sovereignty statements in line with our conceptualization. In a final step, each statement was attributed to one of the following policy areas: immigration, security, EU and foreign policy, Austrian values, education, social policy, work, economy, agriculture and environment, administration and state reform, as well as direct democracy. Claims spanning various policy areas were recorded on multiple sovereignty dimensions to accurately capture their complexity, but attributed to the best-fitting policy area to allow for meaningful interpretation; in the overall analysis, these crossovers were taken into account.

Analysis: the sovereignty claims of the Austrian radical right and mainstream right

To answer the question of how the radical-right Freedom Party (FPÖ) and the mainstream-right People's Party (ÖVP) (re)constructed Austrian sovereignty, this section analyses their manifestos and leadership speeches between 2013 and 2017 in terms of national, economic, and popular sovereignty. This analysis focuses on (a) the scope of the sovereignty claims in each dimension – by assessing the number and type of policies to which these claims were connected, and (b) the degree to which these sovereignty claims were made, indicating how intensely the party and its leaders argued for an increase in Austrian sovereignty. The degree of the claim is assessed by investigating whether specific quantities are set or changed, the presence of urgency or pertinence in the language, and the level of finality in the proposed solution. References to the speeches indicate the speech number and are attributed to the exact date in the appendix.

Reconstructing sovereignty: the Austrian Freedom Party

Reporting the results of the manifesto analysis for 2013 and 2017, Table 1 shows in which policy areas the FPÖ made sovereignty claims and whether the scope and degree of these claims increased over time. In both manifestos, the FPÖ addressed all three dimensions of sovereignty, claiming an expansion of sovereignty is necessary. Furthermore, the scope and degree of these claims, meaning the extensiveness of the policies and the intensiveness of the claims, have increased in most policy areas.

On the dimension of national sovereignty claims, the FPÖ focused on two broad areas. First, it stresses the importance and need to defend specific Austrian values. Command of the German language is defined as a condition for entrance into the education and social systems whereas Austrian cultural identity was emphasized for protecting Austrian media

Table 1. Areas with sovereignty claims in FPÖ manifestos.

Issue area	2013	2017	Development of sovereignty claims
National sovereignty			
Immigration	German language Islam Asylum	German language Islam Asylum Border control Foreign students	More (scope)
Values	German language	Cultural identity Media Multiculturalism Islam	More (scope & degree)
Education	German language Foreign students	German language Foreign students	Same
Agriculture	–	Religious slaughter	More (scope & degree)
EU	Turkey	Turkey Human Rights EU borders Austrian neutrality	More (scope & degree)
Security	Austrian neutrality	Austrian neutrality Border control National defence Foreign criminals	More (scope & degree)
Economic sovereignty			
Immigration	Welfare Social housing	Welfare Social housing Asylum seekers	More (scope & degree)
Education	–	Foreign students University fees	More (scope & degree)
Social Policy	Welfare Social housing Tax benefits	Welfare Social housing Health insurance	Same
Labour	No opening of job market	Sectoral closure	More (degree)
EU	ESM/EFSF EU debt Contributions Job market	ESM/EFSF Immigration	Less (scope)
Agriculture	–	Autarky	More (scope & degree)
Economy	Subsidies	Free-trade agreements Protection of cash	More (scope & degree)
Popular sovereignty			
Direct Democracy	Referendums Veto-referendums	Referendums Veto-referendums Swiss model	More (scope & degree)
EU	–	Renationalization of competences No EU army	More (scope & degree)
Economy	–	Free-trade agreements	More (scope & degree)

and guarding against the cultural influence of Islam. Such sentiments feature heavily in the speeches of Herbert Kickl and Heinz-Christian Strache, who claim immigration reduces the quality of life for Austrians, leads to crime ('parallel societies') (Strache 24), and introduces an alien Muslim population incompatible with Austrian society (Kickl). National sovereignty claims also concern 'Austrian interests' with respect to broader institutional influences. Central to this is the constitutionally enshrined principle of Austrian (military) neutrality, which is to be protected from non-neutral European foreign policy decisions and a push to build up national defence capabilities. While neutrality was a central issue in both 2013 and 2017, the latter manifesto expanded on this issue in a reaction to the refugee crisis after 2015. National Austrian interests now also required protection through a fortified European border and, where that was not possible, through a strong national border defence.

The economic sovereignty dimension focused on the protection of the socio-economic interests of individual Austrians and the Austrian economy in general. In both manifestos, the FPÖ expressed grave concern about how foreigners impinge on the socio-economic interests of Austrian citizens, especially by competing for jobs and accessing public welfare. While the 2013 manifesto saw European migrants mainly in terms of draining finite Austrian resources, the 2017 manifesto expanded the circle of 'undeserving others' to asylum seekers. The protection of Austrian workers against foreign competitors was a particular focus for Kickl, who used very militaristic language when linking economic sovereignty to matters of 'national defence' (Kickl 3) and labour-market policy to 'self-defence' (Kickl 4). Secondly, the FPÖ was concerned about the protection of the Austrian economy from the harmful effects of EU or international policy measures. Here, we find that sovereignty claims changed. In 2013 the main focus lay with the EU's monetary and financial policies that were depicted as draining resources from the Austrian economy and the taxpayer. This included concerns about the extent of the Austrian contribution to the EU budget and the liabilities incurred due to the different financial stabilization mechanisms adopted by the Eurozone. Kickl also emphasized the need to protect 'Austrian economic standards' from those of the EU (Kickl 1). The 2017 manifesto adds calls for building up Austria's agricultural self-sufficiency, staying out of international trade agreements like TTIP, and resisting an alleged EU plan to abolish cash money.

On the popular dimension of sovereignty, the FPÖ calls for expanding direct democracy in both manifestos, but goes into greater detail in 2017. Only in 2017 do the demands for more direct democracy include a list of specific institutional changes aimed at bringing the Austrian system closer to the Swiss model. Similarly, both Kickl and Strache call for Austrians to be given the opportunity to decide on specific EU initiatives (i.e. leaving the Euro, introduction of EU tax, etc.) through a binding referendum. However, neither the manifesto nor the speeches state explicitly that plebiscitary democratic mechanisms should generally *replace* parliamentary decision-making. In fact, Strache stresses that these measures are meant to complement parliamentary democracy (Strache 11).

The 2017 FPÖ manifesto also adds the demand for the renationalization of certain decision-making competences and warns against any further transfers of authority away from Austria. Although introduced only in the most recent manifesto, these points have been prominent features in FPÖ speeches for much longer. For instance, Strache rejected the idea of a 'European central state' (23), opposing transferring any competences in immigration policy to the EU (Strache 7). He also called for the Austrian government to reclaim the authority to control its own borders (e.g. Strache 12, 13, 14, 16). Both Kickl and Strache made frequent claims based on popular sovereignty when accusing the government of failing to represent the Austrian people. Kickl called the government the 'stooge' and 'extended work bench' of the European Commission (Kickl 2), and also 'agents' of the European Union (Kickl 3). Strache criticized the Austrian government's agreement with the German government, calling them 'the parrot of [Angela] Merkel' (Strache 8). In sum, FPÖ speeches address both the national and supranational level in their Eurosceptic and anti-establishment rhetoric. This finding underscores the populist nature of the Freedom Party and marks a distinction to the ÖVP.

In sum, the FPÖ makes sovereignty-related claims in a wide variety of policy areas. Central to both national and economic sovereignty claims is that the FPÖ is very clear about privileging the perceived interests of the core, traditional Austrian population over many economic, social and cultural concerns. When it comes to popular sovereignty, the FPÖ calls for national political decision-making and considers it generally superior to international decision-making. While the FPÖ also demands expanding plebiscitary opportunities, we do *not* find evidence that the FPÖ claims opposition to parliamentarism itself.

Reconstructing sovereignty: the Austrian People's Party

Table 2 shows the policy areas in which the ÖVP made sovereignty claims in its 2013 and 2017 manifestos. One strong contrast to the FPÖ manifesto is immediately discernible. In 2013, the ÖVP had a number of policies that called for a continued absence or further yielding of Austrian sovereignty (marked in italics in Table 2), which are also prevalent in the leaders' speeches. With the exception of the creation of a European border defence force, these types of 'anti'-sovereignty claims have vanished in the 2017 manifesto. Furthermore, both the degree and the scope of existing sovereignty claims increased in the documents. In the speeches, the shift towards more sovereignist claims has been subtler, even though Kurz has clearly granted these statements more attention and appears more Eurosceptic than his predecessors.

On the level of national sovereignist claims, Table 2 shows a clear increase in scope and degree from 2013 to 2017. While the basic sovereignist claims, especially the importance of the German language and Austrian values, were present in 2013, these were extended in the 2017 document. We find an even stronger shift in the leaders' speeches, which first focused on anti-sovereignist claims in favour of an open country in the 'Austrian humanist tradition', arguing that to suggest otherwise would be an 'insult' (Mitterlehner 20). Furthermore, Lopatka (31) made clear that Islam, just like Judaism, was part of Austrian society. Over time, these claims were replaced by clear sovereignist statements focusing on the need for immigrants to learn German and adopt Austrian values (e.g. Kurz 1), the struggle of integration (Mitterlehner 29), and the dangers of Islamic parallel societies (Kurz 3). By 2017, the ÖVP's national sovereignist claims resemble those of the FPÖ.

In the manifesto, we find a similar shift in the degree and scope of sovereignist claims on the economic-sovereignty dimension. The 2013 manifesto highlights the socio-economic advantages of European integration and international trade agreements, arguing for a further strengthening of these ties and thus less national sovereignty, but more general welfare. This was also – and remained over time – the position in the leaders' speeches. For instance, both Mitterlehner (32, 40) and Lopatka (23) argued extensively for the benefits of free-trade and international climate agreements. Lopatka (22) went so far to deny prioritizing Austrian economic well-being in connection to the EU sanctions against Russia. In the 2017 manifesto, the ÖVP made a strong economic-sovereignist turn, stressing the need to protect the Austrian job market and welfare system from immigration, but also calling for changes within the European system to protect the Austrian state budget. The only corresponding aspects in the speeches was a move away from arguing that immigrants are economically advantageous (Lopatka 40), to focusing on pressures created for the welfare system (but not the job market) (Kurz 3, Lopatka 48 & 51).

SOVEREIGNISM AND POPULISM

Table 2. Areas with sovereignty claims in ÖVP manifestos.

Issue area	2013	2017	Development of sovereignty claims
National sovereignty			
Immigration	German language Clear rules for immigration	German language Illegal immigration Pre-selection of refugees EU asylum system	More (scope & degree)
Values	Booklet with Austrian values for immigrants	Austrian values education & cultural initiatives Christian symbols Islam Foreign political influence in civil society	More (scope & degree)
EU & foreign policy	Effective embassies Modern Austria Specialized Turkey partnership	Refugees in region Christian persecution No to Turkey in EU Austrian and EU border control	More (scope & degree)
Security	–	Border controls Foreign influence in civil society	More (scope & degree)
Education	–	German language Austrian values	More (scope & degree)
Economic sovereignty			
Immigration	*Welcome culture**	Mandatory social service	More (scope & degree)
Education	*Internationalization of tertiary education* *Coordinate research*		More (less anti-sovereignty claims)
Social	–	Welfare	More (scope & degree)
EU & foreign policy	*0.7 per cent for development budget* *Use EU for Austrian companies*	Smaller EU Commission & bureaucracy EU contributions Sanctions against Russia	More (scope and degree)
Agriculture	*EU agriculture policy* Austrian standards in treaties	–	Less (scope & degree)
Economy	Made in Austria Energy autarky No tax money for banks *International cooperation*	Fight tax fraud Protection of cash No zero-interest policy	Same (equivalent)
Work	*Access for skilled labour*	Points system Regulate duration	More (scope & degree)
Popular sovereignty			
Immigration	–	No voting rights for foreigners	More (scope & degree)
EU and foreign policy	*Austria as mediator* More democracy in EU *Subsidiarity* (both *pro-EU* and national parliament) *More EU law assertion* *More competencies EU commission* *EU bank regulation* *EU solutions and harmonization*	More democracy in EU Subsidiarity (mainly national)	More (degree)
Security	*EU foreign and security policy (incl. army)*	*EU level border control defence organization*	More (fewer anti-sovereignty claims)
Environment	*International climate protection*		More (fewer anti-sovereignty claims)
Trade	*International trade rules* *Common EU energy market*		More (fewer anti-sovereignty claims)
Direct democracy	At EU level Referendums Online direct democracy	Referendums	Less (scope)

Note: *anti-sovereignty claims are in italic; for a detailed table see appendix.

On the popular-sovereignty dimension, we find a shift from many anti-sovereignty claims in 2013 to some sovereignty claims in 2017, which was again more strongly evident in the manifesto than in the speeches. This is particularly the case for the distribution of decision-making competences.[1] In the 2013 manifestos, we find multiple claims for strong(er) inter- and supra-national decision-making, both as general principles and with regards to trade, the environment, and security policies. The same claims were present in the leader speeches that focused on the superiority of international trade and environmental agreements and the centrality of the European Union decision-making for Austria. Mitterlehner argues 'the EU, that is us' (20); the EU brings advantages but also duties, and the centrality of solidarity (e.g. Mitterlehner 30, also Lopatka 44). The ÖVP leaders stressed that solutions should preferably be found at the EU level and national-level decisions were 'a step back' (Lopatka 3). In 2017, the ÖVP dropped most of these anti-sovereignist claims. Further, the 2017 manifesto included popular-sovereignist claims, however, only when stressing national decision-making in reference to the subsidiarity principle. In the speeches, we find one central instance of a clear sovereignist turn: While Lopatka stressed the centrality of EU-level decision-making, he first argued that the involvement of national legislatures was important (21, 24), but over time replaced the parliaments with 'strong nation states' (61, 68). However, there are no explicit claims to re-nationalize decision-making competences.

In sum, therefore, on all three dimensions the ÖVP made a switch from anti-sovereignist claims in 2013 to sovereignist claims in 2017. This turn is especially pronounced on the national and economic sovereignty dimensions, where the ÖVP under Kurz adopted strong positions and rhetoric for protecting and strengthening the native Austrian people. This turn coincides with a leadership change from Mitterlehner and Lopatka – who were sceptical towards cooperation and convergence with the FPÖ – to Kurz, who was and is substantially more open to the right. This change is not only reflected in the manifesto, but also in the content of the leadership speeches. While we had not expected the ÖVP to stress economic sovereignty as much as it did, our findings confirm our theoretical assumption that the populist FPÖ puts more emphasis on popular sovereignty.

Thus, analysing the parties' manifestos and leader speeches yielded several insights regarding the construction of sovereignist claims. For one, we find that both parties make sovereignty claims on all three dimensions of sovereignty, with the exception of the ÖVP on the populist dimension. Moreover, we observe a shift towards sovereignist values on all three dimensions that cuts across issue areas. Particularly with respect to the EU level, the FPÖ's emphasis on lower-level decision-making ('handing back the power to the people') has grown stronger and touches upon multiple other areas such as trade negotiations or immigration policies and asylum. The ÖVP, on the other hand, reduced anti-sovereignist claims (e.g. open labour-market policies, EU solutions and harmonization, etc.), which parallels the trend towards more nationally-oriented policy positions. Lastly, it is the ÖVP that appears to have undergone the most radical reorientation, abolishing their pro-European stance in favour of more anti-multiculturalist and nationalist positions. This transition subsumes a broad array of policy areas under a sovereignist narrative and even stretches to usually unsuspicious matters such as education policy and the internationalization of tertiary education.

Austrian voters' attitudes and opinion shifts towards sovereignist values

In our analysis of the demand side of how populism relates to sovereignism, we proceed from the same theoretical assumptions laid out earlier. Thus, we expect populist-party voters to support all three sovereignty claims, but to show a special affinity for popular sovereignty. By contrast, we would hypothesize finding the least support for this last category among conservative party voters. To answer this question, we used data from the Austrian national election survey in 2013 and 2017 (Kritzinger et al., 2016; Wagner et al., 2018) and identified survey items that tap into each of the three sovereignty dimensions: national, economic, and popular sovereignist sentiments. Table A3 in the appendix summarizes the details. In the following, we use boxplot graphs and ANOVA analyses (see Table A4, appendix) to investigate whether (a) the voters of the ÖVP, FPÖ, and all other parties have significantly different views, and (b) whether ÖVP voters' preferences shifted towards FPÖ voters' preferences.

The first measure, shown in Figure 1, investigates voters' preferences regarding economic sovereignty values. The statement suggesting that 'migrants take away Austrian jobs' taps into respondents' belief that immigration is a threat to the socio-economic well-being of Austrians. Voters' responses in 2013 reveal no significant differences in means between ÖVP supporters and those who cast their votes for other parties, while FPÖ voters had significantly more negative views. In 2017, the picture looked fundamentally different: First, all three voter groups – especially FPÖ voters and other party voters – became less convinced of the negative job impact of immigrants, which is surprising, but may be a result of the strong state of economic recovery in Austria when compared with the situation five years earlier. Second, ÖVP and FPÖ voters converged significantly, to the extent that their means were completely aligned. However, this is not a consequence of

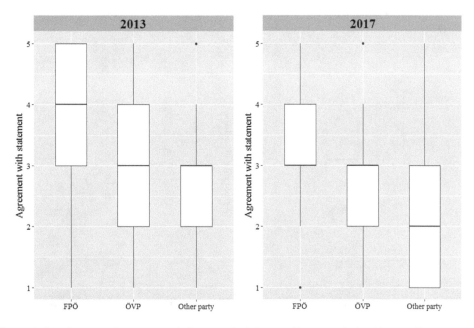

Figure 1. Austrian voters' response to 'migrants take jobs away' by party choice. Note: 1: disagree completely; 5: agree completely; $N = 1161$ (2013), $N = 2935$ (2017).

ÖVP voters becoming more economically sovereignist, but of FPÖ voters (and other party voters) becoming less so.[2] Thus, the shift of the ÖVP towards more sovereignist claims is not an answer to their voters' attitudinal 'development'.

Figures 2 and 3 investigate the voters' preferences on the national dimension of sovereignism. In terms of voters' attitudes to European integration, Figure 2 shows that both ÖVP and FPÖ voters became more negative towards the EU from 2013 to 2017. In 2013, there was no significant difference in means between the voters of the ÖVP and other parties, but such a difference did exist in 2017. The difference in means between ÖVP and FPÖ voters was significant in both years and decreased only slightly, from 2.7 to 2.0 scale points. Thus, we find some convergence between the two parties' sets of voters, which is in line with the direction of the ÖVP's sovereignty claims in 2017.

Figure 3 shows a similar result for the perceived cultural impact of migration on Austrian values and traditions. Even though the attitudes of ÖVP voters and those of other parties were already statistically distinguishable in 2013, the gap was larger in 2017 and, at the same time, ÖVP voters' positions had moved closer to those held by FPÖ supporters: both far-right and conservative voters perceived the cultural impact of migration to be very extensive in 2017. Thus, we do find convergence between these two voter groups on this indicator corresponding to the party's behaviour: FPÖ voters became even stronger in their already established conviction, while ÖVP voters moved in the same direction.

Finally, for the popular dimension of sovereignty claims, we only have data available from 2017 and, thus, can draw limited inferences. Figure 4 shows the proportion of policy areas that respondents want handled at the national level. FPÖ voters prefer on average that 74.1 percent of policies should be decided upon only by the national government (as opposed to 'together within the EU'), while ÖVP voters preferred for 62 percent of all areas to be

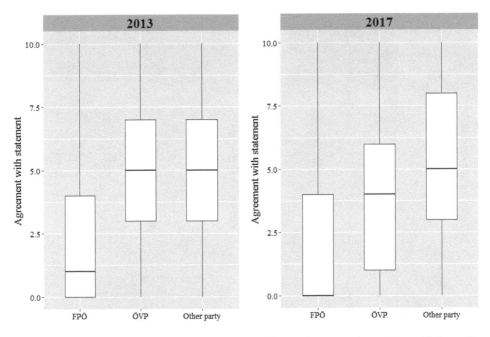

Figure 2. Austrian voters' attitudes to European integration by party choice. Note: Higher values denote more positive attitudes; $N = 1141$ (2013), $N = 2765$ (2017).

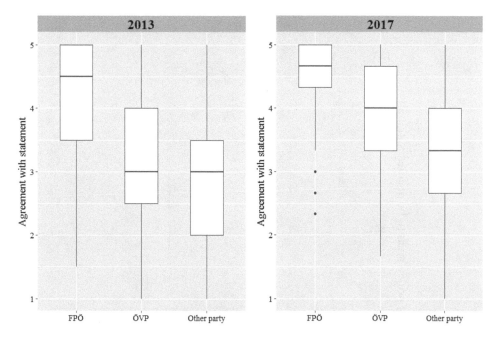

Figure 3. Austrian voters' view on the cultural impact of migration by party choice. Note: Higher values denote more negative attitudes; N = 2162 (2013), N = 2797 (2017).

decided only nationally. By contrast, only slightly more than half of all policy areas (53 percent) should be handled nationally according to the supporters of other parties. This suggests there are differences as to how exclusively national decision-making should unfold. While the FPÖ mirrors its voters' strong preference for far-reaching national competences, the ÖVP's electorate seem to be stronger proponents of 'taking back the control' than is their party.

While Figure 4 displays preferences for moving decision-making power from the international to the national level, Figure 5 shows the preferences for moving this power from elected officials to the people via direct democracy. While ÖVP and other party voters take a neutral position on this question, favouring neither more nor less direct democracy, FPÖ voters have a significantly higher preference for direct democratic decision-making. Thus, FPÖ claims for the introduction of the 'Swiss model' are in line with their voters' preferences. The ÖVP made comparatively weak claims regarding direct democracy in 2017, which seem in line with their voters' neutral position.

In sum, the attitudes of the two parties' voters shifted markedly on all three dimensions from 2013 to 2017. This development only partially matches the parties' claims and partially runs counter to their developments. Thus, voter preferences regarding sovereignty cannot consistently explain the party claims. On the national dimension, ÖVP voters moved considerably closer to FPÖ voters. This corresponds to a trend at the party level, which has resulted in a strong campaign emphasis on 'Austrian values' and 'tradition'. However, no such developments took place on the economic dimension of sovereignism where it was FPÖ voters that turned more moderate, thus bringing their attitudes closer to those of conservative voters. By contrast, ÖVP voters maintained stable centrist attitudes. By comparison, the ÖVP's manifesto, and to a lesser degree the leader speeches, showed a much greater swing towards sovereignist claims. This split is likely caused by the perceived trade-off

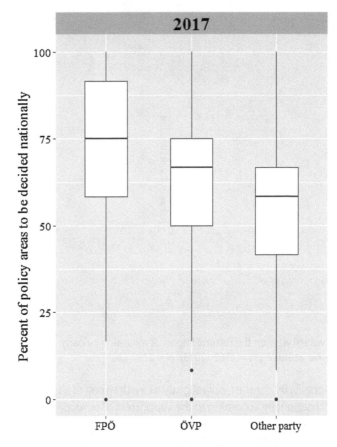

Figure 4. Austrian voters' view on the adequate level of decision-making per policy area by party choice. Note: 0: all policy areas should be decided together within the EU; 100: all policy areas should be decided only nationally; $N = 2520$.

between liberal, open-market positions and nationalist, culturally isolationist values. In order to provide a relatively coherent campaign message, the party may have sought to combine these two aspects. Likewise, our analysis of the popular sovereignty dimensions, for which we only had data from 2017, reveals a rather large gap between FPÖ and ÖVP voters. Conservative voters appear less supportive of forms of direct democracy and the 'Swiss model' than are their far-right counterparts. This matches the parties' positions, but such a neutral stance on popular sovereignty is unlikely to cause conflicts with the FPÖ.

Conclusion

Decades of globalization and denationalization have generated sentiments of profound discontent, culminating in counter reactions that come in some form of populist attitudes and actors (Kriesi et al., 2006). Populist radical-right and, more recently, centre-right parties across Western political systems have therefore rediscovered and reclaimed seemingly lost values in a nostalgic yearning for self-determination (Hainsworth, 2016; Meijers, 2017). In Austria, as elsewhere, this has not left the character of party competition unaffected. Specifically, the perception that Austrian sovereignty had been undermined

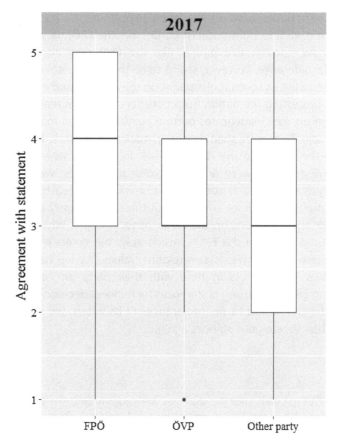

Figure 5. Austrian voters' preference for direct democracy by party choice. Note: Higher values denote more support for direct democracy; sample size: $N = 2825$.

resonated strongly with many voters. Consequently, whereas the FPÖ had been a constant advocate of Austrian sovereignty (despite adopting a somewhat softer tone in its 2017 election campaign), the 'New' ÖVP under Sebastian Kurz was now also discovering the salience of a 'take back the control' programme.

As no systematic approach to analyse these developments had been undertaken, this article examined the respective election manifestos of the ÖVP and the FPÖ from 2013 and 2017. It also examined the party leadership speeches during this period, identifying claims that support or counter national, economic, and popular sovereignty. In doing so, we conceptualized the relationship between radical-right populist and conservative actors and their voters, on one hand, and the three dimensions of sovereignism on the other. Furthermore, we analysed voter data to see whether the shifts at the party level corresponded to those at the citizens' level. We find that both parties used a range of policies to underscore their sovereignty claims. While the populist FPÖ covered all three sovereignty dimensions, the ÖVP focused on national and economic sovereignty. Following a change in the party leadership, the ÖVP renounced its anti-sovereignist and pro-European claims and instead adopted many of the FPÖ claims rooted in national and economic dimensions of sovereignty. At the same time, the ÖVP has avoided becoming more populist, as it did not adopt the Manichean notion between the 'good' people and the 'bad' others. Thus, sovereignist claims are central to right-populist parties like the FPÖ, they are not exclusive to them. As we show, conservative parties like the ÖVP may also adopt sovereignist claims. The crucial difference, however, seems to be the popular sovereignism dimension. While the ÖVP increased its sovereignist claims on the national and economic dimensions, aimed mainly at protecting the nation from outsiders, it did not really embrace claims of popular sovereignism, which advocates putting political decision-making directly into the hands of the people. This, more than anything, marks the contrast to the populist FPÖ.

Turning from the supply to the demand side and testing whether the sovereignist claims of the ÖVP and FPÖ were driven by voter preferences, we find in the second part of our analysis that there is considerable overlap between the FPÖ's sovereignty claims and the preferences of its voters on all three sovereignty dimensions. The gap between the ÖVP and its voters, on the other hand, is larger. While the ÖVP narrowed the programmatic distance to the FPÖ considerably, the voters of the former did not support *all* of these shifts towards sovereignist values. As we had suggested at the outset, ÖVP voters seemed less in tune with their party on economic sovereignty, despite expressing generally strong preferences for national decision-making and national values. Thus, if the ÖVP reacts to the preferences of its voters, we might see them tone down some of their sovereignist stances again.

Notes

1. Neither the ÖVP manifesto nor the speeches were majorly concerned with direct democratic decision-making. While the 2013 manifesto included some calls for such tools, the 2017 manifesto only mentions referendums which, in turn, were rejected by Lopatka in one speech (speech 86).
2. This result is confirmed by Figure A1 (appendix), which compares the 2017 voter groups' responses to whether immigration had negative impact on the Austrian economy. FPÖ voters agree with this statement significantly more than ÖVP voters.

ORCID

Reinhard Heinisch ⓘ http://orcid.org/0000-0002-0019-2423
Annika Werner ⓘ http://orcid.org/0000-0001-7341-0551
Fabian Habersack ⓘ http://orcid.org/0000-0001-7792-1447

References

Akkerman, T., de Lange, S., & Rooduijn, M. (2015). Inclusion and mainstreaming? Radical right-wing populist parties in the new millennium. In T. Akkerman, & S. De Lange (Eds.), *Radical right-wing populist parties in Western Europe: Into the mainstream?* (Extremism and democracy) (pp. 1–29). London: Taylor and Francis.
Bale, T. (2008). Turning round the telescope. Centre-right parties and immigration and integration policy in Europe. *Journal of European Public Policy*, *15*(3), 315–330.
Bale, T. (2010). Cinderella and her ugly sisters: The mainstream and extreme right in Europe's bipolarising party systems. *West European Politics*, *26*(3), 67–90.
Basile, L., & Mazzoleni, O. (2019). Sovereignist wine in populist bottles? An introduction. *European Politics & Society*. doi:10.1080/23745118.2019.1632576

Betz, H., & Meret, S. (2012). Right-wing populist parties and the working class vote. In J. Rydgren (Ed.), *Class Politics and the Radical Right* (pp. 107–121). London/New York: Routledge.

Brubaker, R. (2017). Why populism? *Theory and Society, 46*(5), 357–385.

Dolezal, M. (2008). Austria: Transformation driven by an established party. In H. Kriesi, E. Grande, R. Lachat, M. Dolezal, S. Bornschier, & T. Frey (Eds.), *West European politics in the age of globalization* (pp. 105–129). Cambridge: University Press Cambridge.

Downs, A. (1957). An economic theory of political action in a democracy. *Journal of Political Economy, 65*(2), 135–150.

Hafez, F. (2014). Shifting borders: Islamophobia as common ground for building pan-European right-wing unity. *Patterns of Prejudice, 48*(5), 479–499. doi:10.1080/0031322X.2014.965877

Hainsworth, P. (2016). *Politics of the extreme right: From the margins to the mainstream. History and politics in the 20th century.* London: Bloomsbury Publishing.

Heinisch, R. (2002). *Populism, proporz, pariah: Austria turns right: Austrian political change, its causes and repercussions.* New York: Nova Science Pub Incorporated.

Heinisch, R., McDonnell, D., & Werner, A. (2018). *Equivocal Euroscepticism: How some radical right parties play between 'reform' and 'rejection'.* Paper prepared for the IPSA World Congress, Brisbane, 21–26 July 2018, pp. 1–20.

Kitschelt, H. (1995). Formation of party cleavages in post-communist democracies theoretical Propositions. *Party Politics, 1,* 447–472.

Kriesi, H.-P., Grande, E., Lachat, R., Dolezal, M., Bornschier, S., & Frey, T. (2006). Globalization and the transformation of the national political space: Six European countries compared. *European Journal of Political Research, 45*(6), 921–956.

Kritzinger, S., Johann, D., Thomas, K., Glantschnigg, C., Aichholzer, J., Glinitzer, K., … Wagner, M. (2016). *AUTNES online panel study 2013.* Vienna: AUSSDA. doi:10.4232/1.12647

Krzyżanowski, M. (2017). Discursive shifts in ethno-nationalist politics: On politicization and mediatization of the "refugee crisis" in Poland. *Journal of Immigrant & Refugee Studies, 4*(2), 1–21.

Luif, P. (1995). *On the road to Brussels: The political dimension of Austria's, Finland's, and Sweden's accession to the European Union* (Vol. 11). Vienna: Braumüller.

Luo, C.-M. (2017). The rise of populist right-wing parties in the 2014 European parliament: Election and implications for European integration. *European Review, 25*(03), 406–422.

Meguid, B. M. (2005). Competition between unequals: The role of mainstream party strategy in niche party success. *American Political Science Review, 99*(3), 347–359.

Meguid, B. M. (2010). *Party competition between unequals: Strategies and electoral fortunes in Western Europe. Cambridge studies in comparative politics.* Cambridge: Cambridge University Press.

Meijers, M. J. (2017). Contagious Euroscepticism: The impact of Eurosceptic support on mainstream party positions on European integration. *Party Politics, 23*(4), 413–423.

Moffitt, B. (2016). *The global rise of populism: Performance, political style, and representation.* Stanford: Stanford University Press.

Pytlas, B. (2015). *Radical right parties in Central and Eastern Europe: Mainstream party competition and electoral fortune.* London: Routledge.

Schumacher, G., & van Kersbergen, K. (2014). Do mainstream parties adapt to the welfare chauvinism of populist parties? *Party Politics, 22*(3), 300–312.

Spruyt, B., Keppens, G., & van Droogenbroeck, F. (2016). Who supports populism and what attracts people to it? *Political Research Quarterly, 69*(2), 335–346.

Stanley, B. (2008). The thin ideology of populism. *Journal of Political Ideologies, 13*(1), 95–110.

Taggart, P. (2000). *Populism.* Buckingham: Open University Press.

Wagner, M., Aichholzer, J., Eberl, J.-M., Meyer, T., Berk, N., Büttner, N., … Müller, W. C. (2018). *AUTNES online panel study 2017.* Vienna: AUSSDA. doi:10.11587/I7QIYJ.

Should we stay or should we join? 30 years of Sovereignism and direct democracy in Switzerland

Sean Mueller ⓘ and Anja Heidelberger

ABSTRACT
Sovereignism is on the rise. Defending a nation's political autonomy, fortifying its international borders, preserving cultural identity and shielding the domestic economy from the adverse effects of globalization are core demands. Often contained within research on populism or Euroscepticism, this article conceptualizes Sovereignism as an ideology on its own. Three separate, yet connected, dimensions of Sovereignism are distilled: political, which negates sharing ultimate decision-making with supranational bodies; economic, which concerns market access and trade liberalization; and cultural, which regards foreign citizens as a threat to national culture. Empirically, we track the impact of sovereigntist arguments on citizens' voting behaviour, by analysing all 68 referendums held in Switzerland between 1983 and 2016 concerning supranational integration, economic ties, immigration, asylum and/or cultural demarcation. We rely on a multilevel analysis of post-vote survey replies to show how the three dimensions interact with party politics, values and contextual factors. Our main finding is that all three dimensions of Sovereignism continue to matter, but that values and party politics have in the meantime absorbed a big part of their impact.

Introduction

In November 2018, Swiss voters rejected a constitutional amendment entitled 'Swiss Law Instead of Foreign Judges (Self-Determination Initiative)'.[1] If accepted, the Swiss constitution would have taken precedence over international law and jurisprudence (except jus cogens); conflicting international treaties would have had to be renegotiated and, if necessary, cancelled. Furthermore, the Federal Tribunal would only have been permitted to consider international agreements that had passed the optional referendum test, which is, for example, not the case for the European Convention on Human Rights (BR 2017, p. 5405). Launched by the right-wing populist Swiss People's Party (SVP) and ultimately defeated, this specific proposal nevertheless throws into sharp focus the much wider issue of Sovereignism as

- An ideology protecting and defending a state's sovereignty against supranationalism and global constitutionalism (Rensmann, 2016)

- A critique of (the expansion of) international law as lacking democratic credentials on procedural grounds: unelected and foreign judges, obscure and distant bureaucrats (Pollack, 2017)
- A critique of the substance of trans-national law as contradicting national political culture and values, based on the presumed particularity of one's own legal regime (Resnick, 2008, p. 35)
- A reaction to globalization, in general (Alles & Badie, 2016, p. 18), and the declining importance of state borders vis-à-vis goods, capital, services and workers, in particular (Kallis, 2018, p. 295ff.; Ivaldi & Mazzoleni, 2018; Helleiner & Pickel, 2005).

Consequently, defending a nation's political autonomy and independence, maintaining democracy domestically, strengthening state borders, preserving its cultural identity and shielding its economy from the adverse effects of globalization are core demands put forth by sovereigntists (Hobolt, 2016, p. 1262). Often contained within research on nationalism, right-wing populism or Euroscepticism, this article examines Sovereignism as an ideology on its own merits, although there remain significant conceptual and partisan overlaps (De Spiegeleire et al., 2017).

The next two sections define and conceptualize Sovereignism in general. Three dimensions in particular are distilled. The *political* dimension relates to sharing decision-making with supranational organizations such as the UN, the WTO or the EU. The *economic* dimension concerns trade liberalization, access to domestic and international markets, and labour rights. The *cultural* dimension refers to whether foreign nationals (including expats, asylum seekers, *sans papiers*, refugees and cross-border workers) are regarded as a threat, or as enrichment for the nation's cultural identity and community life.

Sections 3 and 4 focus on Sovereignism in Switzerland, a country at the heart of Europe with a rich tradition of referendums on all sorts of policy questions. We study the nature and evolution of Sovereignism through 68 referendums held between 1983 and 2016. All of them had to do with supranational integration, immigration, asylum, cultural demarcation and/or economic relations. So, unlike studies that analyse EU-related referendums only (Hobolt, 2009; Hug, 2002; Mendez et al., 2014), or which operationalize sovereignty more narrowly through international recognition and 'core competences of the state' (Mendez & Germann, 2018, p. 145), we widen both our empirical and our conceptual scope. This allows us to compare different policy issues related to Sovereignism and track citizen behaviour over more than 30 years, since such referendums occur quite regularly and within the same overall setting (all are binding and Swiss-wide). We then rely on a multilevel analysis of post-vote survey responses to specific arguments to show how the three dimensions interact with individual characteristics, party politics, populism, nationalism and context. The general question answered through this process is the following: Is there such a phenomenon as 'Sovereignism', meaning a set of interrelated opinions all defending a nation-state's political, economic and/or cultural sovereignty? And, more specifically: does it have an influence on individual voting behaviour?

Defining Sovereignism

Sovereignism is an ideology that places a nation-state's sovereignty above all else (Spiro, 2000, p. 9). Sovereignty here refers to the 'Westphalian' notion of 'territoriality and the exclusion of external actors from domestic authority structures', as well as full control over cross-border flows of 'goods, persons, pollutants, diseases and ideas' (Krasner, 1999, p. 12, 20). Sovereigntists accept international agreements only if they serve to buttress ultimate and unrestricted decision-making by their citizens in and over their territory. Yet they are agnostic as to *how* citizens exert their sovereignty domestically, that is to say, via representative, majoritarian, federal and/or direct democracy (Resnik, 2008). Global, supranational and trans-national rules are found wanting both in content and procedure (Pollock, 2017). Consequently, by no means are sovereign powers to be transferred beyond the state (Goodhart & Bondanella Tanichev, 2011, p. 1049).

Sovereignism comes in two variants: principled and pragmatic.[2] For *principled* sovereigntists, maintaining or restoring a state's *de facto* and de jure independence is the goal and not merely an instrument for achieving better policies. They firmly believe in 'the uncontested primacy of national-level politics' (Kallis, 2018, p. 299). In his latest speech at the UN, for example, Donald Trump (2018) put it thus: 'Sovereign and independent nations are the only vehicle where freedom has ever survived, democracy has ever endured or peace has ever prospered. And so, we must protect our sovereignty and our cherished independence above all'. Consequently, 'We will never surrender America's sovereignty to an unelected, unaccountable, global bureaucracy. [...] We reject the ideology of globalism, and we embrace the doctrine of patriotism' (Trump, 2018).

Pragmatic sovereigntists, in turn, are more selective, flexible and merely temporary sovereigntists. They use sovereigntist language to pursue either a libertarian, deregulatory agenda, if located on the political right (Moravcsik, 2000, p. 293, 301), or aim for as much protection of fundamental rights and socio-economic regulation as possible, if on the left (Pollock, 2017, p. 8). They object to international agreements and supranational institutions only for as long as these obstruct policies in line with their own preferences, and/or until such bodies have themselves become more inclusive, participatory and transparent (Pollock, 2017; Steger & Wilson, 2012).

Neoconservative sovereigntists, for example, have no problem with enabling corporations to sue democratic governments for investment losses, but object to the jurisdiction of the International Criminal Court (Resnik, 2008). European Socialists, Greens and Liberals, in turn, have objected to trade and other agreements with the USA and Canada on the grounds of rights violations of EU citizens (Pollock, 2017, p. 8). Yet they want the EU to accede to the European Convention of Human Rights (e.g. European Parliament, 2016; cf. also Goodhart & Bondanella Tanichev, 2011, p. 1048). Similarly, in 1992 the Swiss Greens objected to the accession of Switzerland to the European Economic Area (Senti, 2012), as did the SVP, – but for entirely different reasons, namely on pragmatic grounds and not as a matter of principle (e.g. Bornschier, 2010).

Right-wing populist parties are principled sovereigntists. They oppose foreign standards *tout court* (Keohane et al., 2009, p. 3). In their analysis of 16 European populist parties and the US Republicans, as well as Trump's campaign speeches, De Spiegeleire et al. (2017, p. 76ff.) found that all 18 actors advocated 'taking back or maintaining national control of policy-making'. 17 actors wanted to 'reinstate or reinforce border controls' and 16 to 'increase national control over inter/supranational organizations', with the remaining parties not having a clear position. All but the Movimento Cinque Stelle are right-wing populists; left-wing populists such as Syriza and Podemos did not score sufficiently sovereigntist to be analysed (De Spiegeleire et al. 2017, iv and personal correspondence).

Table 1 places principled Sovereignism alongside exclusive nationalism and right-wing populism, on the left, and market and justice globalism, on the right. The former two concepts are related in that they similarly use the inclusion-exclusion mechanism, although what is sealed off from outside interference is more the national community as opposed to state sovereignty, for the first, whereas right-wing populism excludes the 'impure elite' (both domestic and foreign) from the 'pure people' (Mudde, 2007, p. 23). The main enemies of principled Sovereignism are not other nations or foreigners (people), but rules: international standards and covenants, and especially tribunals such as the European Court of Human Rights (ECtHR), are seen as obstacles to the full realization of national self-determination. Trans-national law and its actors (e.g. the other 46 judges on the ECtHR) are not only alien, far away and ignorant, but also non-political, unelected and thus lacking democratic legitimacy (Benhabib, 2016, p. 126; Moravcsik, 2000, p. 306ff.), hence the label of 'foreign judges' used by the Swiss People's Party when targeting the ECtHR through their 'self-determination initiative' (Schubarth, 2017; BR, 2017; also Keohane et al., 2009, pp. 21–22).

The right-hand side of Table 1 displays two prominent, but antagonistic targets of Sovereignism. Market globalism refers to the neoliberal attempt to create a single, world-wide market for goods, services, capital, ideas and people, while justice globalism is equally encompassing in territorial reach but 'place[s] the needs and rights of people before corporations [...] to secure a just and sustainable future for people and the planet' (Steger & Wilson, 2012, p. 449). Pragmatic sovereigntists oppose *either* market *or* justice globalism, adducing *either* procedural reasons – such as lack of transparency – *or* substantive objections – such as not enough, or too much freedom for persons to move (Resnik, 2008; Pollock, 2017).

Both types of globalism conceive of humans as morally and legally equal individuals regardless of residence and citizenship (Benhabib, 2016, p. 113). Principled Sovereignism, in turn, regards every human as a member of just one political community: their nation-state (Goodhart & Bondanella Tanichev, 2011, p. 1050). Its plea is 'for a retreat of nations into their borders' (Alles & Badie, 2016, p. 18; also Kallis, 2018), and the obligations of government lie with 'the majority of our own people' only (cited in Moravcsik, 2000, p. 304). In sum, whereas globalism advocates a post-Westphalian understanding of equality of consumer or citizen rights and worldwide competition or solidarity, principled Sovereignism insists on separation into distinct states and national self-determination – 'there can be no substitute for strong, sovereign, and independent nations' (Trump, 2017).

Table 1. Sovereignism and four related but distinct concepts.

	Exclusive nationalism	Right-wing populism	Principled Sovereignism	Market globalism	Justice globalism
Primary reference	'our' nation	the people	'our' state	the market	justice
Key value	supremacy	purity	self-determination	competition	solidarity
Main enemy	other nations	elite (foreign/domestic)	the supranational	(re-) regulation	corporations
Policy demand	less/no immigration	(more) direct democracy	supremacy of domestic rules	global free trade	global equality
View on borders	closed (for people)		closed (for rules)	open (for capital)	open (for people)

Right-wing populism, excusive nationalism and principled Sovereignism often appear together, for example, in the presidency of Donald Trump, or during the Brexit campaign (Hobolt, 2016, p. 1266). Yet differences remain, most notably regarding policy demands (Table 1). Populists always argue in the name of the people, and hence defend or demand more 'popular' sovereignty, often in the form of referendums (Mudde, 2007, p. 151ff.; a notable exception being the US Republicans, cf. De Spiegeleire et al., 2017, p. 68). Sovereigntists, by contrast, are satisfied with protecting 'state' sovereignty, leaving the precise mode of exercising it domestically open. For example, 'taking back control' during the Brexit campaign meant re-empowering the UK parliament, and not introducing direct democracy all around, which is precisely what the SVP claimed to defend ahead of the November 2018 vote. Nationalists, in turn, defend the supremacy of 'our' nation, and mainly want less or even no immigration. Little do they care, in principle, where the rules governing their community originate. For both sovereigntists and nationalists, then, even a less than fully democratic regime would suffice if only it enabled effective resistance against the outside.

The agnostic position of principled Sovereignism towards democracy also becomes visible when contrasted with the right-hand side of Table 1. In fact, supranationalism *enhances* national democracy if it protects minorities, guarantees fundamental rights, enforces socio-economic security, contains vested interests and promotes deliberation (Keohane et al., 2009; Pollock, 2017; Resnik, 2008). Principled sovereigntists may well acknowledge the limits of supposedly independent policy-making by their nation-state in the face of increasing globalization. Still, they object to internationally agreed solutions or those derived from the jurisprudence of other countries because they violate domestic sovereignty (Goodhart & Bondanella Tanichev, 2011, p. 1065; Resnik, 2008). They object even if that means *worse* policy solutions, *weaker* democracy and *less* protection domestically through higher prices for imported goods, abstaining from multilateral negotiations, and the absence of an external enforcer of rights such as the ECtHR (Moravcsik, 2000, p. 313). We shall henceforth focus on principled Sovereignism.

Dimensions

As with Euroscepticism, nationalism, populism (Bornschier, 2010; Grande & Hutter, 2016; Hobolt, 2016; Hooghe & Marks, 2018; Kriesi et al., 2012; Mudde, 2007) or social science concepts more generally (e.g. Goertz, 2006), Sovereignism possesses several dimensions. The preceding discussion has emphasized three aspects in particular: culture, economy and politics. Although primarily concerned with sovereignty as a legal and political construct, the ideology has both cultural and economic implications when it comes to who should constitute the demos and where potential danger could come from, namely through immigration or lack of economic means of subsistence. We discuss these two first before returning to the political dimension.

Culturally, Sovereignism aims for the protection of a nation's collective identity and peaceful existence against foreign intrusion, rivalry, dilution and crime. The particular traits of the collective identity supposedly under threat can be ethnic (e.g. the national language or religion) or civic (e.g. pride in productivity, institutions or law-abiding modesty). The enemies of cultural Sovereignism, so to speak, are thus less the supranational organizations and regimes, as such, but rather the individuals or groups whom these organizations and regimes permit to enter, stay, work and live in the country. Hence the opposition to the EU's free movement of persons and demands for the re-introduction of border controls. Sovereignism's strategic alliance with exclusive nationalism is most obvious in this dimension (Alles & Badie, 2016, p. 18). A famous image summarizing this aspect is that of the 'Polish Plumber' in France and the UK, who symbolised the openness of the (now intra-EU) border to East-European citizens. The Polish Plumber is, of course, not only Polish but also a plumber, which brings us to consider the second dimension of Sovereignism.

Economically, sovereigntists strive to shield the domestic economy from the adverse effects of globalization, market integration and other countries' competitive advantages (Hooghe & Marks, 2018). Domestic companies and employees and the wealth and products generated by them are intrinsic goods, on the one hand, but also instrumental in that they enable the country to remain independent from the outside world. While the goal of autarky ties it to the agricultural sector and its deep-seated image as both essential food-producers and homeland, protectionism can serve other industries, too, for example the energy and communication sectors. Supranational institutions are again identified as the main culprit. To wit, again, Donald Trump (2018): 'countries were admitted to the World Trade Organization that violate every single principle on which the organization is based. [...] The United States lost over 3 million manufacturing jobs, nearly a quarter of all steel jobs, and 60,000 factories after China joined the WTO. [...] We will not allow our workers to be victimized, our companies to be cheated, and our wealth to be plundered and transferred. America will never apologize for protecting its citizens'.

The cultural and economic dimensions connect Sovereignism to factors that are usually found to influence an individual's propensity to be Eurosceptic (Safi, 2010, p. 107). By contrast, those who either expect or have already experienced personal or collective gains from EU integration are in favour of it: highly skilled, well-educated and cosmopolitan persons with a universalist or European identity (e.g. Safi, 2010, p. 113; also Hobolt, 2016 and Kriesi et al., 2008). Thus, if defensive-exclusive (but not aggressive-expansive) nationalism marks cultural Sovereignism, protectionism and selective state interventionism occupy the economic side. But there is more to the story than simply regarding the supranational as either a threat or opportunity in cultural and/or economic terms. Goods and people are important, but rules matter, too. To a large extent, such concerns for the *political* dimension of sovereignty are driven by real-world developments themselves. These are aptly summarized by Hooghe & Marks (2018, p. 114):

> National sovereignty and its political expression, the national veto, are obstacles to problem-solving, which is why many international organizations pool authority among their member states in quasi-majoritarian decision-making.

Right-wing populist parties almost always use this political dimension most prominently in their manifestos and electoral campaigns. They share a deep-seated and principled resistance to international legal regimes of all kind, from the UN through the EU 'super-state', to the ECtHR (De Spiegeleire et al., 2017) and the International Criminal Court (Pollock, 2017; Resnik, 2008). Moreover, the Swiss People's Party (SVP), for example, defends the right of the Swiss citizenry to decide policy questions directly, regularly, bindingly and – most importantly – in an unrestricted manner (Albertazzi & Mueller, 2013, pp. 362–363). While such direct-democratic absolutism is unique in comparison to the US, British or

Hungarian Sovereignism, the logic of argumentation is not: democratic nation-states are built on popular sovereignty, so the people should remain sovereign in line with *their own* democratic procedures. The rallying cry of Brexiteers, to 'take back control', accordingly refers to parliamentary sovereignty (de Londres, 2017), US sovereigntists emphasize 'foundational American commitments to democratic majoritarianism and [...] federalism' (Resnik, 2008, p. 34), and in Switzerland it is direct democracy.

Why Switzerland? Case and data

The following analyses focus on the case of Switzerland, for two main reasons. First, there is a striking resemblance between sovereigntist discourse and voting behaviour in Switzerland and recent events in the US, the UK and elsewhere (De Spiegeleire et al., 2017). The actors themselves are fully aware of this. For example, when Steve Bannon visited Switzerland in spring 2018, he called the SVP's *de facto* leader, Christoph Blocher, 'Trump before Trump' (Swissinfo, 2018). Similar praise was heaped onto the Swiss way of dealing with the EU by Nigel Farage, then UKIP leader and main advocate of Brexit, on his visit four years prior: 'you lucky people!' (Schoop, 2014). So as other sovereigntists look to be inspired by Swiss developments, it is important to study that context more closely.

That inspiration is both substantive and procedural. Regarding the former, the main aspect to be pointed out is that Switzerland is not a member of the EU, yet has fairly broad access to its single market. Procedurally, what is praised is the fact that citizens get to vote on important policy questions directly, via referendums, and can even set their own (constitutional) agenda in a binding way, via popular initiatives. The main actor to have opposed both further supranational integration and immigration is the SVP, whose ascendancy began precisely with – and due to – its opposition to the European Economic Area (EEA) in 1992 (Kriesi et al., 2005). Direct-democratic instruments have played a key role for the SVP's mobilization, radicalization and issue-ownership strategies (Kriesi et al., 2005).

The second reason why we study Switzerland is that, precisely because of direct democracy, it offers an almost unique opportunity to study the evolution and dimensions of Sovereignism. Every year, several collectively binding, nation-wide referendums are held. Some of them explicitly focus on Sovereignism, such as the aforementioned 'self-determination initiative' rejected in 2018, accession to the EEA, UN membership or immigration caps. Projects concerning Sovereignism differ in the dimensions – political, cultural or economic – that are affected. Since June 1981, referendums have been followed by an official post-vote survey (VOX); amongst others, respondents were asked their opinion on at least four issue-related arguments. Some of these arguments can be assigned to the three dimensions. VOX also includes information on individual vote choice, as well as socio-demographic and socio-psychological factors. This allows us to verify whether and to what extent the various dimensions of Sovereignism have evolved and if and how they have influenced vote choice.

Methodologically, we proceeded in three steps. We first surveyed all the opinions/arguments ever asked by VOX pollsters on all the 259 referendums assessed between June 1981 and June 2016.[3] For every vote, VOX includes between 4 and 19 questions asking for (dis)agreement (expressed from −2 through 0 to +2) with the most important opinions voiced in the campaign leading up to the vote. These arguments had been carefully selected by political scientists in the run-up to the survey. From all the arguments ever posed, we selected those relating to Sovereignism, meaning they had to explicitly relate Switzerland to the outside and allude to a potential threat or opportunity. This left us with 136 arguments on 68 different referendums held between 1983 and 2016, that is to say, on average, some two arguments per referendum on Sovereignism (see Appendix A.1).

Second, we categorized all these sovereigntist arguments as being either political, cultural or economic (see again Appendix A.1). *Political* arguments concern the question of where ultimate decision-making power should lie. For instance, the argument that EEA accession is a stepping-stone towards EU membership offers a political perspective since it has to do with eventually sharing decision-making supranationally. *Cultural* arguments concentrate on differences between Swiss citizens and immigrants or asylum seekers, hence the argument that immigration as such leads to higher criminality is a cultural argument. Finally, *economic* arguments contain assessments about the cost and benefit of international treaties for the Swiss economy – for instance, that the Bilateral Treaties signal the end for Swiss agriculture. Selection and categorization were done by the two authors separately, and disagreements were then resolved consensually. We thus ended up with 60 political, 44 cultural, and 37 economic arguments, bringing the total to 141 (in five cases, an argument was placed into two categories at the same time). Where needed, we recoded the arguments so that higher values indicate greater support for Sovereignism. Using these arguments, we then created three variables, one each for the political, cultural and economic dimensions.

Results

This section assesses whether agreement with arguments associated with cultural, economic and political Sovereignism influenced individual vote choice in Switzerland between 1983 and 2016. If so, can we identify a hierarchy between these three? Are there changes over time? We subsequently run multilevel logistic regressions, since voters and their choices are nested within the different referendums and their attributes.

The *dependent variable* is the self-declared vote choice of respondents. Since we would like this to capture Sovereignism, we recoded vote choice for all proposals that suggested a culturally more cosmopolitan, internationally and economically open, or supranationally integrated course of action (e.g. accession to the UN), so that voting 'yes' now means being in favour of Sovereignism (i.e. voting against UN accession).

As *independent variables*, we use respondents' agreement with the aforementioned pro and contra arguments, which we have ourselves classified as political, cultural, or economic (see also Appendix A.1). We also include the year of each vote in our analysis, to check if and how the impact of the three dimensions has changed over time.

In addition, we include several controls that have been shown to impact individual vote choice. Regarding gender and age, we assume higher support for Sovereignism by men and older people (Hobolt, 2016), whereas when it comes to education, we expect citizens with a lower level of education to prefer more Sovereignism (Sciarini and Tresch, 2009). Territorially, we include respondents' linguistic region, relying on the observation that German-speaking and Italian-speaking Swiss[4] are more sovereigntist than French-speaking Swiss (cf. e.g. Kriesi et al., 1996), and we distinguish between rural and urban areas, assuming rural citizens to prefer more Sovereignism (Scholten, 2014). We also model party preferences, because parties are highly important in the Swiss semi-direct democracy for organizing and mobilizing voters (e.g. Ladner, 2014; Mueller & Bernauer, 2018), and because they exhibit different positions regarding Sovereignism (Trechsel, 2007; Linder & Mueller, 2017). More specifically, we expect SVP supporters to favour Sovereignism more strongly than all others. We also include trust in government, since populist attitudes were argued above to partially overlap with Sovereignism (McLaren, 2007).[5]

We also make use of attitude variables,[6] which we use to measure *values*. Most importantly, we incorporate an index constructed using self-ascribed positions on three items concerning the integration–demarcation conflict, which is said to be highly important for votes on EU integration and immigration (Kriesi, 1998; Kriesi et al., 2012). We equally include a variable concerning the state-market conflict, which could prove important for the economic side of voting. Finally, we model a variable concerning preferences for federal vs. unitary state solutions, since some aspects of the political dimension of Sovereignism – namely the degree of inter-territorial solidarity, the importance of borders and shared rule areas – resemble centralization at supranational level. However, we do not include the traditional variable on left-right self-positioning, since perceptions by respondents have changed over time.

To control for *vote-specific impacts*, we include a variable on the share of the four major (governing) parties supporting the sovereigntist position. This allows us to see whether Sovereignism is less (or more) pronounced when there is consensus across the political spectrum, assuming that greater endorsement of the sovereigntist position by the elite enhances the probability for a favourable vote. We control for the strength of populist attitudes in a year by aggregating all responses on the integration–demarcation index over a calendar year.[7] Additionally, we take into consideration that quite a few popular initiatives on Sovereignism were formulated and supported solely by the SVP. We control for these special cases using a dummy variable for popular votes in which the SVP alone favoured the sovereigntist position. The position of the Federal Council (the Swiss executive) is also included since for many citizens it functions as an important and trusted cue-giver. Finally, we control for the type of the vote, that is to say, whether it is a popular initiative demanding constitutional change, a facultative referendum against a specific Act of Parliament, or a mandatory referendum in case of constitutional amendments decided by Parliament. While the initiative and mandatory referendum both relate to the federal constitution, both the initiative and facultative referendum are launched from outside Parliament. The type of the vote matters because of the different success rates associated with them (Kriesi, 2005; Linder & Mueller, 2017).

Additionally, we need to make sure that we are actually measuring the impact of the arguments themselves and not the impact of the mere *supply* of these arguments. Otherwise it could be the case that any effects we are able to detect derived from the fact, that in some years, sovereigntist votes mainly concerned cultural aspects, while in other years, it was votes on the political side of Sovereignism that dominated. Indeed, Figure 1 shows that the number of arguments across the three dimensions varies strongly over time, but that the three dimensions largely meander together. We thus also take differences in the supply of arguments into account, on the assumption that the number of arguments captures the saliency of any given dimension.

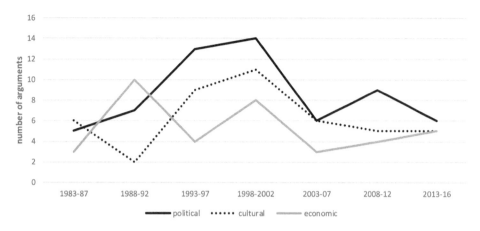

Figure 1. Number and type of sovereigntist arguments per referendum, 1983–2016.

The argument variables can only be included in the analysis sequentially, since there are missing values for all proposals where such questions were not asked. Their impact is thus conditional on proposals where an effect has already been expected by the designers of the questionnaire. We need to keep this in mind when interpreting our findings.

Table 2 shows the results of our multilevel logistic regression models, with the projects as grouping variable at level 2. We see that all of the arguments significantly and positively influence individual vote choice. Models 2–4 show how agreeing with any of the three types of arguments predicts Sovereignism. Cultural arguments have a slightly stronger effect than the other two, but the size of the impact of the three dimensions on the vote choice regarding sovereigntist questions is more or less identical. Thus speaking *only* of culture or only of culture *and* economics when talking about Sovereignism would mean to neglect a substantial part of the phenomenon. In turn, the supply of political, cultural or economic arguments in the last five years before a given popular vote does not significantly affect individual vote choice.[8]

Model 5 includes all three dimensions simultaneously and thus only considers six popular votes.[9] This allows us to compare the respective impact of the three dimensions, albeit only in a handful of (important) projects. We can thus see that in these specific cases – which either had to do with the EU or concerned successful SVP initiatives – economic arguments had a stronger effect on vote choice than cultural or political arguments, although the latter two also prove significant. Once more, then, all three dimensions matter.

Table 2 also shows several other significant determinants of sovereigntist voting. Traditional determinants like gender, education, language, party preference and trust in the national government all matter in the expected directions. At the level of votes, neither the size of the pro-camp, nor the distinction of projects into those only supported by the SVP vs. all others significantly affects vote choice. The probability of a sovereigntist vote is only greater when a larger coalition supports the proposal and the economic dimension is concerned.

If we next include our value variables (see Table A.2 in the Appendix), which we could not for our main models as they were only assessed after 1994, we see a significant and positive effect for demarcation preferences, as well as partly for federalism. In these

SOVEREIGNISM AND POPULISM

Table 2. Multilevel logistic regressions on vote choice concerning sovereigntist proposals.

	Model 1	Model 2	Model 3	Model 4	Model 5
Political arguments		0.72***			0.48***
		(0.01)			(0.04)
Supply of political arguments		0.09			
		(0.05)			
Cultural arguments			0.80***		0.59***
			(0.02)		(0.04)
Supply of cultural arguments			−0.02		
			(0.08)		
Economic arguments				0.74***	0.79***
				(0.02)	(0.05)
Supply of economic arguments				0.17	
				(0.10)	
Age	0.07	−0.04	0.16*	−0.07	−0.28
	(0.04)	(0.06)	(0.07)	(0.07)	(0.17)
Sex	−0.16***	−0.17***	−0.19***	−0.20***	−0.11
(0=male, 1=female)	(0.03)	(0.04)	(0.04)	(0.05)	(0.11)
Language: French	−0.13***	−0.15***	−0.22***	−0.15**	−0.22
(base group: German)	(0.03)	(0.05)	(0.05)	(0.05)	(0.13)
Language: Italian	0.22***	0.37***	0.27***	0.22*	1.11***
(base group: German)	(0.05)	(0.07)	(0.08)	(0.09)	(0.20)
urban – rural	−0.05*	−0.10*	−0.08	−0.00	−0.15
(base group: urban)	(0.03)	(0.04)	(0.05)	(0.05)	(0.12)
Level of education	−0.13***	−0.15***	−0.13***	−0.10***	−0.23***
	(0.01)	(0.01)	(0.01)	(0.01)	(0.04)
Trust in government	−0.66***	−0.95***	−0.82***	−0.44***	−1.22***
	(0.03)	(0.04)	(0.04)	(0.05)	(0.11)
Party: SP	−2.01***	−2.06***	−2.22***	−1.65***	−2.68***
(base group: SVP)	(0.05)	(0.08)	(0.09)	(0.09)	(0.24)
Party: FDP	−1.19***	−1.30***	−1.41***	−0.74***	−1.77***
(base group: SVP)	(0.05)	(0.08)	(0.09)	(0.09)	(0.23)
Party: CVP	−1.26***	−1.46***	−1.59***	−0.77***	−1.72***
(base group: SVP)	(0.06)	(0.09)	(0.10)	(0.10)	(0.26)
Party: Green	−1.96***	−1.97***	−2.29***	−1.40***	−2.10***
(base group: SVP)	(0.09)	(0.13)	(0.15)	(0.15)	(0.38)
Party: other party	−1.17***	−1.30***	−1.32***	−0.87***	−1.78***
(base group: SVP)	(0.05)	(0.07)	(0.08)	(0.08)	(0.22)
Party: no party preference	−1.16***	−1.25***	−1.27***	−0.97***	−1.77***
(base group: SVP)	(0.04)	(0.07)	(0.08)	(0.08)	(0.22)
size of pro-camp	0.58	−0.25	2.14	2.89*	2.92
	(0.46)	(0.58)	(3.42)	(1.21)	(3.05)
coalition: SVP vs. others	0.18	0.44	−0.18	0.30	−−
(base group: other coalition)	(0.19)	(0.24)	(0.80)	(0.40)	
government recommendation	0.87**	1.59**	0.21	−0.74	−−
	(0.33)	(0.52)	(2.47)	(0.89)	
facultative referendum	0.07	0.06	0.10	0.08	−1.31**
(base group: initiative)	(0.16)	(0.26)	(0.31)	(0.34)	(0.54)
mandatory referendum	−0.14	0.05	0.21	−0.17	−1.63
(base group: initiative)	(0.23)	(0.35)	(0.43)	(0.81)	(1.71)
counterproposal	−0.59	−−	−−	0.42	−−
(base group: initiative)	(0.62)			(0.84)	
year	−0.01	−0.03	−0.01	0.00	−0.06
	(0.01)	(0.02)	(0.02)	(0.02)	(0.08)
Constant	0.23	−0.22	0.28	−1.27	2.30
	(0.26)	(0.50)	(0.74)	(0.98)	(1.94)
N (respondents)	35,449	19,897	16,460	14,020	3883
N (projects)	70	37	30	27	6
AIC	40,444	18,427	14,445	13,146	2284
BIC	40,639	18,617	14,630	13,335	2428

***$p < 0.001$, **$p < 0.01$, *$p < 0.05$, −: variable dropped because of missing variance.

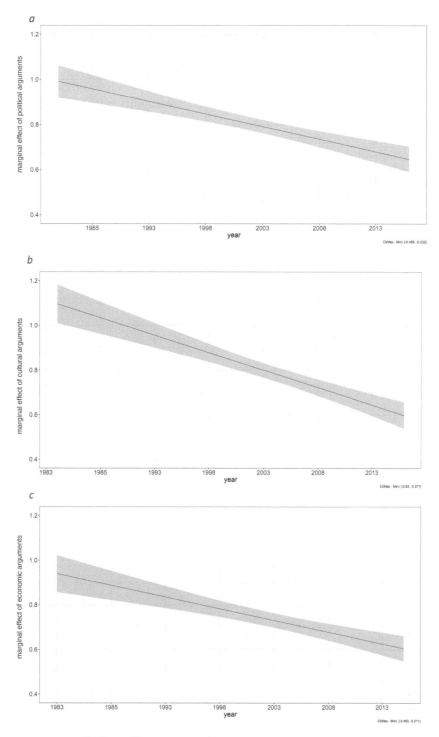

Figure 2. a–c: Marginal effects of sovereigntist dimensions over time.
Note: Values on the y-axis reflect the size of the effect of political, cultural and economic arguments on vote choice.

same models we also include our populism variable, which, however, only significantly impacts vote choice for proposals possessing either a cultural or economic dimension. All three dimensions of Sovereignism retain their positive and significant effects on vote choice of roughly equal magnitude when controlling for those values.

However, we detect no temporal effect on vote choice, neither without (Table 2) nor with the value variables included (Table A.2). Sovereigntist decisions have thus not become more or less probable over the course of these 30 years. However, since public discourses on nation-state sovereignty and immigration (Hooghe & Marks, 2018) have indeed changed over time, along with party activism and mobilization strategies (Hoeglinger, 2016), we might expect a dynamic impact from the different arguments on vote choice. We thus model moderating effects between time and type of

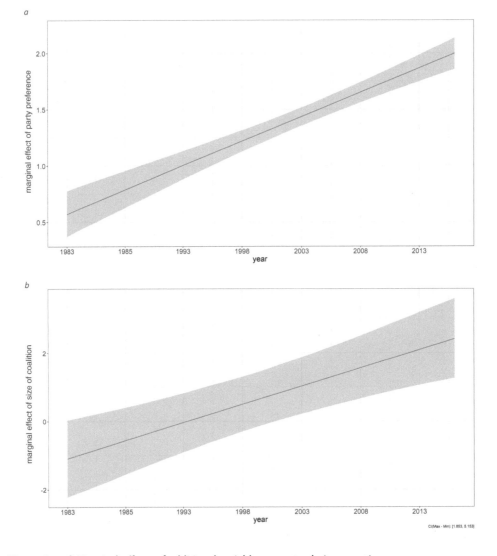

Figure 3. a–f: Marginal effects of additional variables on vote choice over time.

Note: Values on the y-axis reflect the size of the effect on vote choice.

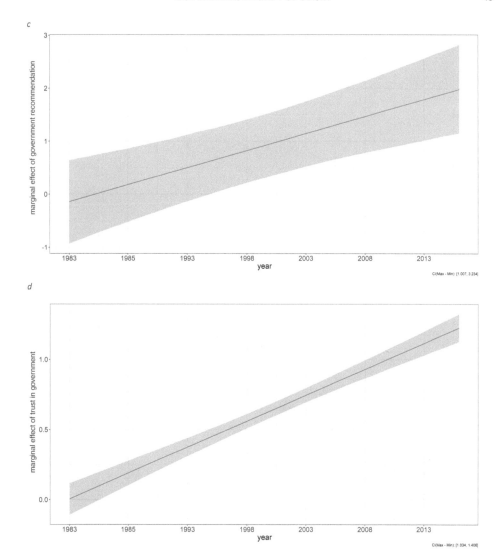

Figure 3. Continued.

arguments. Figure 2(a–c) indeed demonstrates that the impact of all three dimensions on sovereigntist voting has declined over time. In the 1980s, the cultural and political dimensions affected vote choice about equally strongly, but the effect of political arguments decreased slightly more over time and ends up lowest. Economic arguments initially had a somewhat smaller effect than the other two. However, the economic effect did not decrease as steeply and finishes on a par with culture. These findings apply more or less identically to all three linguistic regions of Switzerland (not shown).

Additional analyses show that while the three argumentative dimensions have lost some of their effect on vote choice, cues as well as values have in turn gained in importance. Figure 3(a–f) shows that preferences for the SVP, the size of a coalition in favour of Sovereignism, government recommendations and trust in government as well as integration–demarcation and centralism–federalism have all affected vote

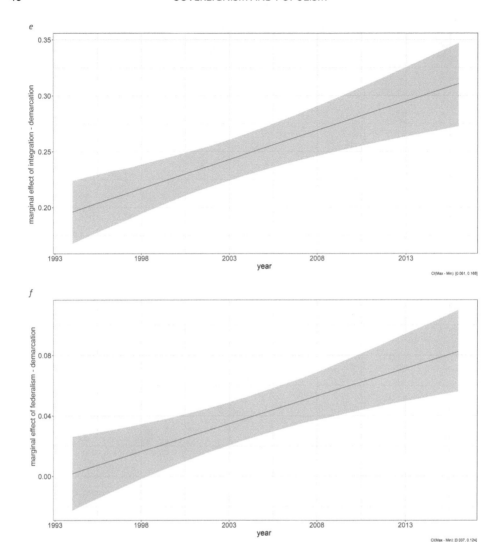

Figure 3. Continued.

choice more strongly over time. This coincides with the often-stated assumption that most Swiss citizens have developed stable predispositions on immigration and EU accession – and thus also on Sovereignism – over time (Milic et al., 2014). That makes them rely less on specific arguments and more on long-term attitudes. What started as a series of vote-specific arguments related to different dimensions of social life has therefore been rebundled into a specific worldview that gives preference to either nation-state sovereignty or international integration in all its facets. We interpret this to mean that not only the arguments, but also the three dimensions have lost some of their impact on Sovereignism over time: the more important stable attitudes and values for individual decision-making, the less relevant the specific issue voted upon.

Conclusion

This article has argued for Sovereignism to be a distinct ideology fighting for or defending nation-state sovereignty. Like so many other social science concepts, sovereignty and Sovereignism possess different dimensions:

1. Where sovereignty relates to cultural identity by delimiting and collectively marking a group of persons (the nation), Sovereignism defends that group from intrusion by non-nationals with different customs, values, or markers.
2. Where sovereignty relates to the economy by defining companies, workers and consumers operating on a fixed territory (the state), Sovereignism strives to assure their prosperity, stability, and success at all costs.
3. Where sovereignty relates to politics by defining those entitled to participate in collectively binding decision-making (the demos), Sovereignism defends that group from outside interference by foreign rules and rule-makers alike.

Using survey data on individual voters on a total of 68 Swiss referendums over more than 30 years has allowed us to measure, verify and analyse the evolution and impact of these three dimensions. Our main finding is that all three types of arguments matter for individual vote choice even after controlling for a range of other factors, including values and attitudes.

Given that the literature has so far largely subsumed politics within *either* the cultural *or* the economic struggle for identity and resources, or argued for politics to be *the result* of their interplay, let us dwell some more on the political dimension. The SVP's 'self-determination initiative' rejected in November 2018 is a paradigmatic expression of that side of Sovereignism. While the Swiss government argued that international treaties are the very result of national sovereignty (BR, 2017, p. 5357), the SVP viewed both the direct-democratic and civic rights of Swiss citizens jeopardized by unaccountable supranationalism and technocratic legalism. Thus although the argument that the non-Swiss ('foreign') judges sitting in Strasbourg are less democratic *because* of their citizenship might be interpreted in a cultural manner, the initiative was eminently political since it argued for the protection of the content and status of the Swiss Constitution (Argumentarium, 2018, p. 4, 8). That strongly resembles Trump's (2018) 'America is governed by Americans' and the Brexit slogan to 'take back control' (cf. also De Spiegeleire et al., 2017).

However, we also detected a declining importance of all three dimensions of Sovereignism – measured through approval with the respective arguments – on vote choice over time. In turn, cues such as political party preference or government recommendations, as well as the more stable values regarding integration–demarcation have become more important for individual decisions. Sovereignism is thus not necessarily a new phenomenon, but what might have changed is its (re-)discovery and manifold use by political actors, notably right-wing populists and nationalists.

Where does all this leave us? Undisputedly, Sovereignism has marked not only direct-democratic, consociational, small and trade-dependent Switzerland, but is also present in representative, majoritarian, large and relatively trade-independent democracies such as the UK and the US. It often serves as one of the argumentative backbones of both nationalism and populism, for example when complaining about international institutions being unaccountable to citizens, distant technocrats hollowing out domestic governance, or waning border control causing an influx of foreigners, drugs and crime (usually conflated into one). However, after momentous events such as the UK voting to leave the EU and an isolationist being elected US president, in the hope not least to restore full 'parliamentary sovereignty' and renegotiate treaties to better serve 'the national interest', Sovereignism clearly deserves to be studied on its own. Looking not just at a few, but at 68 referendums over more than 30 years has allowed us to do exactly that.

The main takeaway message of broader interest from this article is the following. Individual attributes and values such as gender, education and international openness matter for whether the supranational, post-Westphalian world is regarded as a dangerous threat or an enriching opportunity. At the same time, the demarcation–integration conflict and party preferences also play a role. However, it might be precisely Sovereignism's political grain of truth, namely that most supranational institutions *are* less democratic in character than nation-states (Goodhart & Bondanella Tanichev, 2011, p. 1053; Moravcsik, 2000, p. 312; but see Keohane et al., 2009) that explains why its appeal has gone far beyond the core electorate of nationalists or populists *pur et simple*. Only by also knowing of the political dimension of Sovereignism are we able to fully understand such retreats into the nation-state.

Notes

1. E.g. https://www.bk.admin.ch/ch/d/pore/va/20181125/index.html [26.11.2018].
2. We thank one of the journal's reviewers for drawing our attention to this.
3. See http://fors-nesstar.unil.ch/webview [01.10.2018]. Path: "VOXIT -> projects -> vote -> variable description -> III. arguments for the decision". In total, 304 referendums were held in that period (BFS 2018). Of the 297 votes surveyed by VOX, no arguments were asked for 38 votes, leaving us with 259.
4. The position of Italian-speaking Swiss compared to the German-speaking and French-speaking Swiss has changed over the years (e.g. Mazzoleni, 2017).
5. Note that the contradiction between shoring up mistrust in the current government as representing a 'corrupt elite' and defending one's state – and by implication, that very same governing elite – is one that is never really resolved by populist sovereigntists.
6. Unfortunately, attitude questions were only assessed from 1994 onwards.
7. This is far from a perfect measure for populism, but since arguments on demarcation are an important part of (right-wing) populist rhetoric, it does at least help in identifying phases of strong appeal to populist arguments.
8. Leaving out the supply variables reduces the size of the coefficients of the three dimensions only marginally, and they all remain strongly significant.
9. These are: EEA accession (6.12.1992), Bilateral Agreements with the EU (21.5.2000), extension of free movement of persons (25.9.2005), continuation and extension of free movement of persons to Romania and Bulgaria (8.2.2009), ban on minarets (29.11.2009), and the initiative 'against mass immigration' (9.2.2014).

ORCID

Sean Mueller ⓘ http://orcid.org/0000-0003-4369-1449

References

Albertazzi, D., & Mueller, S. (2013). Populism and liberal democracy: Populists in government in Austria, Italy, Poland and Switzerland. *Government & Opposition*, *48*(3), 343–371.

Alles, D., & Badie, B. (2016). Sovereignism in the international system: From change to split. *European Review of International Studies, 3*(2), 5–19.

Argumentarium. (2018). *Argumentarium für die Abstimmung vom 25. November zur Selbstbestimmungsinitiative.* At https://www.selbstbestimmungsinitiative.ch/argumente/ [12.11.2018].

Benhabib, S. (2016). The new Sovereignism and transnational law: Legal utopianism, democratic scepticism and statist realism. *Global Constitutionalism, 5*(1), 109–144.

BFS – Bundesamt für Statistik [Federal Statistical Office]. (2018). *Referendum results, 1848*–2018. At https://www.bfs.admin.ch/bfs/en/home/statistics/politics/popular-votes.assetdetail.6067242.html [1.10.2018].

Bornschier, S. (2010). Integrating the Defense of traditional Communities into the libertarian-authoritarian divide: The role of the Swiss people's party in the redefinition of cultural conflicts. In S. Hug, & H. Kriesi (Eds.), *Value change in Switzerland* (pp. 121–141). Lexington: Lenham.

BR – Bundesrat [Federal Council]. (2017). *Botschaft zur Volksinitiative «Schweizer Recht statt fremde Richter (Selbstbestimmungsinitiative)» vom 5. Juli 2017.* Berne: Federal Council. At https://www.admin.ch/opc/de/federal-gazette/2017/5355.pdf [1. November 2017].

De Londers, F. (2017). The new Sovereignism: what it means for human rights law in the UK. *LSE blog*, http://blogs.lse.ac.uk/brexit/2017/10/24/the-new-Sovereignism-what-it-means-for-human-rights-law-in-the-uk/ [1 October 2018].

De Spiegeleire, S., Skinner, C., & Sweijs, T. (2017). *The Rise of Populist Sovereignism: What it is, where it comes from, and what it means for International security and defense.* The Hague Centre for Strategic Studies, at https://hcss.nl/report/rise-populist-sovereignism-what-it-where-it-comes-and-what-it-means-international-security [1 October 2018].

European Parliament (2016). *Resolution on the situation of fundamental rights in the European Union in 2015.* At http://www.europarl.europa.eu/sides/getDoc.do?type=TA&language=EN&reference=P8-TA-2016-0485 [1 October 2018].

Goertz, G. (2006). *Social science concepts: A user's guide.* Princeton: Princeton University Press.

Goodhart, M., & Bondanella Tanichev, S. (2011). The new sovereigntist challenge for global governance: Democracy without sovereignty. *International Studies Quarterly, 55*, 1047–1068.

Grande, E., & Hutter, S. (2016). Beyond authority transfer: Explaining the politicization of Europe. *West European Politics, 39*(1), 23–43.

Helleiner, E., & Pickel, A. (2005). *Economic nationalism in a globalizing world.* Ithaca, NY: Cornell University Press.

Hobolt, S. B. (2009). *Europe in question: Referendums on European integration.* Oxford: Oxford University Press.

Hobolt, S. B. (2016). The Brexit vote: A divided nation, a divided continent. *Journal of European Public Policy, 23*(9), 1259–1277.

Hoeglinger, D. (2016). *Politicizing European integration: Struggling with the Awakening Giant.* New York: Palgrave Macmillan.

Hooghe, L., & Marks, G. (2018). Cleavage theory meets Europe's crises: Lipset, Rokkan, and the transnational cleavage. *Journal of European Public Policy, 25*(1), 109–135.

Hug, S. (2002). *Voices of Europe: Citizens, referendums, and European integration.* Lanham: Rowman & Littlefield.

Ivaldi, G., & Mazzoleni, O. (2018). *The Radical Right's Politics of Economic Populism and Sovereignism: A comparison between the French Front National (FN) and the Swiss People's party (SVP).* Paper presented at the 4th Prague Populism Conference, May 2018.

Kallis, A. (2018). Populism, Sovereignism and the unlikely re-emergence of the territorial nation-state. *Fudan Journal of the Humanities and Social Sciences, 11*(3), 285–302.

Keohane, R. O., Macedo, S., & Moravscik, A. (2009). Democracy-enhancing multilateralism. *International Organization, 63*, 1–31.

Krasner, S. D. (1999). *Sovereignty: Organized hypocrisy.* Princeton, NJ: Princeton University Press.

Kriesi, H. (1998). The transformation of cleavage politics: The 1997 Stein Rokkan lecture. *European Journal of Political Research, 33*(2), 165–185.

Kriesi, H. (2005). *Direct democratic choice: The Swiss experience.* Lenham: Lexington Books.

Kriesi, H., Grande, E., Lachat, R., Dolezal, M., Bornschier, S., & Frey, T. (2008). *West European politics in the age of globalization (Vol. 6)*. Cambridge: Cambridge University Press.

Kriesi, H., Helbling, M., Grande, E., & Dolezal, M. (2012). *Political conflict in Western Europe*. Cambridge: Cambridge University Press.

Kriesi, H., Lachat, R., Selb, S., Bornschier, S., & Helbling, M. (2005). *Der Aufstieg der SVP: Acht Kantone im Vergleich*. Zürich: Verlag Neue Zürcher Zeitung.

Kriesi, H., Wernli, B., Sciarini, P., & Matteo, G. (1996). *Le clivage linguistique: Problèmes de compréhension entre les communautés linguistiques en Suisse*. Berne: Federal Statistical Office.

Ladner, A. (2014). Politische Parteien. In P. Knöpfel, Y. Papadopoulos, P. Sciarini, A. Vatter, & S. Häusermann (Eds.), *Handbuch der Schweizer Politik* (pp. 361–389). Zürich: NZZ Libro.

Linder, W., & Mueller, S. (2017). *Schweizerische Demokratie* (4th ed.). Bern: Haupt.

Mazzoleni, O. (2017). *Les défis du régionalisme politique en Suisse: Le Tessin et ses relations avec Berne*. Geneva: Slatkine.

McLaren, L. (2007). Explaining mass-level Euroscepticism: Identity, interests, and institutional distrust. *Acta Politica, 42*(2-3), 233–251.

Mendez, F., & Germann, M. (2018). Contested sovereignty: Mapping referendums on sovereignty over time and space. *British Journal of Political Science, 48*(1), 141–165.

Mendez, F., Mendez, M., & Triga, V. (2014). *Referendums and the European Union: A comparative enquiry*. Cambridge: Cambridge University Press.

Milic, T., Rousselot, B., & Vatter, A. (2014). *Handbuch der Abstimmungsforschung*. Zürich: Verlag Neue Zürcher Zeitung.

Moravcsik, A. (2000). Conservative idealism and international institutions. *Chicago Journal of International Law, 1*(2), 291–314.

Mudde, C. (2007). *Populist radical right parties in Europe*. Cambridge: Cambridge University Press.

Mueller, S., & Bernauer, J. (2018). Party unity in federal disunity: Determinants of decentralized policy-seeking in Switzerland. *West European Politics, 41*(3), 565–593.

Pollack, M. (2017). The new, new Sovereignism, or how the European Union became disenchanted with international law and defiantly protective of its domestic legal order. Paper presented at the ISA annual conference, Boston, 22–25 February.

Rensmann, L. (2016). National Sovereignism and global constitutionalism: An Adornian cosmopolitan critique. *Critical Horizons, 17*(1), 24–39.

Resnick, J. (2008). Law as affiliation: "foreign" law, democratic federalism, and the Sovereignism of the nation-state. *I-CON, 6*(1), 33–66.

Safi, K. (2010). Swiss Euroskepticism: Economically or culturally determined? In S. Hug, & H. Kriesi (Eds.), *Value change in Switzerland* (pp. 99–120). Lexington: Lenham.

Scholten, H. (2014). Europapolitik und europapolitische Kampagnen in der Schweiz. In H. Scholten, & K. Kamps (Eds.), *Abstimmungen: Politikvermittlung in der Referendumsdemokratie*. Wiesbaden: Springer VS Verlag.

Schoop, F. (2014). Nigel Farage Superstar. *Neue Zürcher Zeitung*, 4 October, https://www.nzz.ch/zuerich/region/nigel-farage-superstar-1.18397152 [1.10.2018].

Schubarth, M. (2017). Vorrang der EMRK? *Neue Zürcher Zeitung* of 2 November, p. 11.

Sciarini, P., & Tresch, A. (2009). A two-level analysis of the determinants of direct democratic choices in European, immigration and foreign policy in Switzerland. *European Union Politics, 10*(4), 456–481.

Senti, M. (2012). *Europapolitik – Treibstoff der Konservativen*. Zurich: Verlag Neue Zürcher Zeitung.

Spiro, P. J. (2000). The new sovereigntists: American exceptionalism and its false prophets. *Foreign Affairs, 79*(6), 9–15.

Steger, M. B., & Wilson, E. K. (2012). Anti-globalization or alter-globalization? Mapping the political ideology of the global justice movement. *International Studies Quarterly, 56*(3), 439–454.

Swissinfo. (2018). Bannon: 'Blocher is Trump before Trump'. At https://www.swissinfo.ch/eng/speaking-in-zurich_bannon—blocher-is-trump-before-trump-/43952530 [1.10.2018].

Trechsel, A. (2007). Direct democracy and European integration: A limited obstacle? In C. Church (Ed.), *Switzerland and the European Union* (pp. 36–51). London/New York: Routledge.

Trump, D. (2017). Remarks to the 72nd Session of the United Nations General, 19 September. https://www.whitehouse.gov/briefings-statements/remarks-president-trump-72nd-session-united-nations-general-assembly [1.10.2018].

Trump, D. (2018). Remarks to the 73rd Session of the United Nations General, 25 September. https://www.whitehouse.gov/briefings-statements/remarks-president-trump-73rd-session-united-nations-general-assembly-new-york-ny [1.10.2018].

Economic populism and sovereignism: the economic supply of European radical right-wing populist parties

Gilles Ivaldi ⓘ and Oscar Mazzoleni ⓘ

ABSTRACT
While economic issues are increasingly salient in political mobilization by European radical right-wing populist parties, we are still in need of a definition of these parties' economic positions. This paper argues that the economic supply of radical right populist parties is best characterized by a mix of economic populism and sovereignism, which forms the basis of a common mobilization frame. Economic populism refers to defence of the economic prosperity of the 'heartland' against the elite and immigrants. Economic sovereignism is seen, on the other hand, as a means of restoring the people's well-being and the nation's prosperity. To illustrate this argument, we conduct a qualitative analysis of five established European populist radical right parties. We demonstrate that, despite different socioeconomic stances, all parties under scrutiny share a common economic populist sovereigntist frame which claims to defend the self-identified economic interests and well-being of the people. We discuss the implications of our research for the broader understanding of populist mobilization.

The socioeconomic stances of European radical right-wing populist parties (RRPPs) have been extensively discussed in the literature. While there is a consensus that such parties share a common set of cultural and political views, in particular regarding their opposition to immigration, their economic positions are subject to debate among scholars. A first strand of literature deals with the left-right positions of RRPPs on the traditional state-market axis of competition, finding a significant spread of such parties on the whole dimension (Mudde, 2007, p. 123). Another strand of literature focuses on the sociocultural dimension of radical-right politics, linking RRPPs' economic positions to their core radical-right ideology. Some authors emphasize nativism and welfare chauvinism (Afonso & Rennwald, 2018; Mudde, 2007), while others, like Ennser-Jedenastik (2016) and Otjes, Ivaldi, Ravik Jupskås, and Mazzoleni (2018), suggest that RRPPs' economic policies are informed not only by their nativism, but also by their populism and authoritarianism.

While we agree that RRPPs' economic policies relate to their core ideology, we propose a shift in emphasis in the radical-right features informing such parties' economic positions. We argue that RRPPs' political economy is characterized primarily by a combination of 'economic populism' and economic 'sovereignism'. This mix of economic populism and sovereignism forms the basis of a common mobilization frame among RRPPs. Economic populism refers to the idea that the 'true' people's economic well-being is ignored or betrayed by the 'corrupt' elite, and that it should be re-instated. Economic sovereignism, which is linked to such parties' nationalist ideology, is seen as a means of restoring the people's well-being and the Nation's prosperity. Economic sovereignism is essentially a fight for prosperity of the national community, which claims that the nation-state should re-assert its sovereign authority and exclusive control over borders, laws and international interactions, while rejecting supranational influence.

In the first section, we briefly discuss current literature on RRPPs' economic policy and lay down the basis for our framework. Then, to support and illustrate the heuristic interest of our argument, we provide a comparative analysis of five case studies of established radical right populist parties in Western Europe, namely the French Front National (FN, now Rassemblement National, RN), the Swiss People's Party (SVP), the UK Independence Party (UKIP), the Austrian Freedom Party (FPÖ) and the Italian League (La Lega). All of them are prominent examples of radical-right parties, providing a representative mix of RRPPs with different backgrounds, rooted in different political, institutional, socioeconomic and cultural contexts. Using a diverse-case method, we propose a qualitative analysis of those parties' electoral manifestos and economic strategies. Finally, we discuss the implications of our findings for a broader understanding of RRPP supply in political economy.

Linking RRPPs' political economy to populism and sovereignism

Economic issues are becoming increasingly salient for RRPPs, with their economic positions recently receiving more attention (Akkerman, Zaslove, & Spruyt, 2017; Eger & Valdez, 2015; Otjes et al., 2018). As Mudde (2016) acknowledges, 'we must move beyond the dominant focus on the two issues of immigration and European integration, and reflect the broader range of issues the populist radical right parties present to the voters, [including] socio-economic issues' (p. 11). While RRPPs' economic policies have been extensively documented in the literature, there remains a lack of consensus among scholars about such parties' economic positions, and how they may be connected with their core radical-right ideology.

A first aspect of the literature deals with RRPPs' economic left-right positions and how these parties align with the traditional state-market axis of competition. This literature finds diverging economic formulas among RRPP parties. Mudde (2007, p. 123) notes that the RRPP 'spreads a significant part of the whole dimension between the two poles of *laissez-faire* and state economy.' In their seminal work, Kitschelt and McGann (1995) argue that the 'new radical right' mobilized on a combination of culturally authoritarian and economically market-liberal positions, and that this mix of issues represented RRPPs' 'winning formula'. A number of studies continue to link the RRPP to right-wing capitalist economics (e.g. Eger & Valdez, 2015; Kriesi et al., 2008), although it is widely acknowledged that RRPPs have gradually disengaged from market liberalism to adopt a more 'centrist' economic stance during the 1990s (e.g. De Lange, 2007). Recently however, a number of authors have claimed that RRPPs have moved further to the left on the economic axis, adapting their supply of economic policies to the interests and demands of voters with preferences that are culturally right-wing and economically left-wing (Betz & Meret, 2013; Harteveld, 2016; Lefkofridi & Michel, 2014; Van der Brug & Van Spanje, 2009).

Another strand of literature links RRPPs' economic positions to their core radical-right ideology (Afonso & Rennwald, 2018). Mudde (2007) argues that 'for the populist radical right the economy should always be at the service of the nation' and that these parties 'defend a nativist economic program based upon economic nationalism and welfare chauvinism' (p. 137). This second strand of literature focuses essentially on the sociocultural dimension of RRPP mobilization, and follows the characterization of European radical-right populism as 'exclusionary' on cultural issues like immigration (Mudde & Rovira Kaltwasser, 2013, p. 167). Authors like Mudde (2007) and Betz (1994) emphasize nativism and welfare chauvinism as RRPPs' main economic response. Others, like Ennser-Jedenastik (2016) and Otjes et al. (2018), suggest that RRPPs' economic policies are informed not only by their nativism but also by their populism and authoritarianism. According to Otjes et al. (2018), economic authoritarianism refers to the distinction that such parties make between the deserving and the undeserving poor, and the idea that welfare fraudsters should be severely punished, while populism is expressed in economic policies that seek to limit the economic role of the elite and bureaucrats (p. 5-6).

This paper places itself in this second strand of literature. While we agree, however, that RRPPs' economic policies are related to their core ideology, we propose that the focus of analysis should be shifted to emphasize the 'populist' and 'sovereigntist' features of the radical right. We argue that RRPPs' political economy is characterized primarily by a combination of 'economic populism' and economic 'sovereignism'. This mix of economic populism and sovereignism forms the basis of a common mobilization frame among RRPPs, which draws on their core radical-right ideology. This frame functions as a mode of 'attribution' and 'articulation' (Benford & Snow, 2000, p. 615) by identifying a problematic economic condition – *i.e.* the decline of the people's well-being – making attributions regarding who is to blame – *i.e.* elites and outsiders – and articulating an alternative set of policies to enact change – *i.e.* restoring economic sovereignty. In the following sections, we briefly lay out the theoretical background for this approach.

Economic populism and economic sovereignism

For European scholarship, populism remains a controversial term with different meanings (e.g. Heinisch, Holtz-Bacha, & Mazzoleni, 2017; Rovira Kaltwasser et al., 2017). One the most influential perspectives provided by Mény and Surel (2000), then by Canovan (2005) underlines the following features of populism as a challenge to existing representative regimes in Europe: 'the people are the foundation of the community; they have been robbed of their rightful primacy; they must be restored to the proper place and society regenerated' (Canovan, 2005, pp. 81–82).

Thus, in contrast to other conceptualizations like that of Mudde (2007), which suggest a relatively 'static' view of populism, primarily as an attack on the political status quo, populism is seen here not only as a people-centred claim, whereby the people are ignored or betrayed by the elite, but also as a promise of change, a 'project for political renewal' (Urbinati, 2014, p. 151). As Akkerman et al. (2017) suggest, populism remains 'a politics of hope, *i.e.* the hope that where established parties and elites have failed, ordinary folks, common sense and the politicians who give them a voice, can find solutions' (p. 380). Laclau's concept of 'dislocation' (2005, pp. 121–122) emphasizes the 'break with the status quo' by populism. Others, like Hermet (2001) emphasize the 'utopian' impetus of populism inasmuch as it 'systematically exploits the popular dream of an immediate realization of the demands of the masses' (p. 50).

While current concepts of populism do not explicitly refer to the economic dimension *per se*, Mény and Surel (2000), however, implicitly provide an interesting and potentially broader framework to focus on what may be defined as 'economic populism'. Thus, economic populism may be conceptualized by means of three main features: first, the 'true' community of people sharing a common economic destiny, and not only or not necessarily common ethnic or cultural roots and identity; second, the people's well-being, currently fragile or on the decline, and directly at risk; finally, the people's well-being needing to be re-established. For populism, the absolute source of power is unrestricted popular sovereignty. Therefore, in economic terms, one may argue that the restoration of economic sovereignty is seen by populism as the way to re-establish the people's well-being. In other words, without recovering economic sovereignty, any effective restoration of the 'true interests' of the people is simply impossible.

The concepts of 'sovereignty' and 'sovereignism' have seldom been employed in the literature on current European radical-right wing populism. This can partly be explained by the predominance of the concept of nationalism (De Cleen & Stavrakakis, 2017; Mudde, 2007). In fact, sovereignism goes hand in hand with nationalism, however with different emphases (De Spiegeleire et al., 2017). Nationalism refers to the idea that the state and the nation should be congruent, thus emphasizing the nation. In sovereignism, on the other hand, the emphasis is primarily on the state and restoring its authority in the interests of the people in order to reflect their will (Canovan, 2005). Sovereignism typically expresses the idea of 'regaining control' on behalf of a 'redefined' community by 're-spatializing' power (Kallis, 2018, pp. 286–7). It addresses the insulation of the state from society, and demands that 'the sovereignty of the government and the people become coterminous again' (Chryssogelos, 2018, p. 2). In the economic realm, sovereignism seeks to achieve economic prosperity through popular and national re-empowerment. Economic 'sovereignism' has both endogenous and exogenous features. The former concerns the internal conditions required to ensure the welfare of the community, emphasizing such values as the work ethic, while advocating changes in the distribution of resources in favor of the 'true' people. The exogenous features of economic sovereignism focus on protecting the 'true' people from external threats and intrusions. These goals can be achieved through different economic strategies both nationally and at the supranational level, including economic protectionism and welfare chauvinism for instance, combined with market-liberal or more Keynesian demand-oriented domestic economic policies.

Radical right-wing economic sovereignism

Turning to radical right-wing populism, economic sovereignism is embedded in a particular instance of economic populism. RRPPs claim to give priority to the 'national community' in terms of jobs, housing and welfare, while arguing that immigration should be reduced. RRPPs typically embrace welfare chauvinism – that is the belief that access to the welfare state should be restricted to natives (Betz, 1994, pp. 173–174). Additionally, the economic community should be protected from the undeserving poor: those living on benefits or committing welfare fraud, who represent an internal threat to the people's economic well-being and should be excluded from the welfare state (Otjes et al., 2018, p. 5). More generally, within RRP economic populism, both elites and outsiders embody globalisation and European integration, and are considered responsible for the decline or fragility of people's well-being. According to Zaslove (2008), RRPPs' opposition to globalization is based on four components: globalization is elite driven; it limits state sovereignty; it is linked to the growing power of the European Union; it destroys the organic nature of civil society, thereby threatening its natural economic order.

Nonetheless, the impact of globalized processes on party politics is far from being univocal or homogeneous. Political parties may shape different policy responses to pressures from globalization (Lacewell, 2017). Moreover, as Taggart (2000, p. 4) suggests, populism has an 'essential chameleonic quality' that means it can adapt to a variety of issues and contexts. We may thus anticipate variation in the way RRPPs formulate their economic populist sovereignism. In particular, endogenous and exogenous features of economic sovereignism may both be expressed in different policy emphases and orientations that derive their meaning from the particular economic context and political opportunities in which they are deployed. As discussed above, RRPP populist parties may for instance provide market or state-oriented policy prescriptions, and endorse protectionist or free trade policies, according to how they choose strategically to frame their claims of defending or regaining prosperity through the endogenous and exogenous features of economic sovereignism.

Case selection and methodology

To illustrate how economic populist sovereignism expresses itself empirically in the radical right, we develop a qualitative analysis of similarities and differences across a selection of West European populist radical-right parties, seeking to draw inferences from these case studies. As Seawright and Gerring (2008) suggest, case studies imply 'intensive analysis of a small number of units where the researcher's goal is to understand a larger class of similar units' (p. 296). In this paper, we use a diverse-case method and focus on a purposive sample of five established West European populist radical-right parties, namely the French Front National (FN, now *Rassemblement National*, RN), the Swiss People's Party (SVP), the Austrian Freedom Party (FPÖ), the Italian League (Lega) and the UK Independence Party (UKIP). These parties are commonly taken together under the umbrella of the populist radical right (Ford & Goodwin, 2014; Mudde, 2007), thus fitting into our theoretically specified population of inference in terms of their core populist frame and radical-right ideology.

While clearly not covering the entire population of West European RRPPs, this selection provides a mix of parties with different economic traditions and positions, achieving enough variance along other important dimensions that may account for the diversity in their supply of economic populist sovereignism. First, these parties operate in different institutional settings which vary according to the level of centralization of power. Parties, like the SVP, FPÖ and UKIP, operate in federal or decentralized systems, as opposed to more unitary systems of government in Italy and France. Levels of centralization may be a significant factor in such parties' interpretation of their sovereignism, since unitary government may be more conducive to claims of national sovereignty.

Moreover, our selection includes a case of a formerly separatist party with strong ethno-regionalist roots, the Italian Lega, which enables us to assess further the presence of sovereignism as a common frame for RRP mobilization.

Second, our selection includes countries with different levels of integration into the EU. For instance, Switzerland is not a member of the EU and Britain has remained outside the Eurozone, while France and Italy are core founding member states. Differences in EU membership may also influence our parties' supply of economic populist sovereignism and models of resistance against supranational powers.

Third, our five parties of interest assume different positions in their party system. The SVP, League and FPÖ have succeeded in achieving national office, whereas both the FN and UKIP have been excluded from national government. The SVP is traditionally a member of the Swiss federal government according to the 'magic formula' of apportionment of government seats. RRPPs with a governmental profile may be likelier to moderate their populism and sovereignism.

Finally, these parties currently occupy different positions on the economic axis of competition. Otjes et al. (2018) find a significant spread on the left-right economic scale, with the SVP farthest to the right, UKIP, FPÖ and the League right to the center, and the French FN closer to the economic left (p. 285). Thus, these parties provide enough variance to test our proposition that economic populist sovereigntist claims are a common feature of RRPPs, independently of their position on left-right economic issues.

The empirical focus of our paper is on the socioeconomic policies and discourses of our five parties of interest. The analysis is primarily concerned with descriptive rather than causal inference, since it does not seek to identify causal mechanisms accounting for our parties' electoral performance. Our data are drawn mainly from party manifestos – manifestos being considered reliable sources of information on political parties' policy emphases and positions (Marks, 2007). For each case, we focus on the two most recent national elections to illustrate both the salience and coherence of economic populism and sovereignism in our five parties. The list of party manifestos considered in the analysis is presented by election year in Appendix A and all manifestos are referenced in the paper. Other sources – interviews, written statements and speeches by party leaders – are used primarily for illustrative purposes when deemed relevant. These additional sources are listed and referenced in Appendix B.

The variety of empirical sources and selection of parties in this study serve to examine similarities and differences in our RRPPs' economic populism and sovereignism. To account for commonality and variability across our five cases, we look first at the main features of the right-wing economic populist frame – *i.e.* common economic destiny of the 'people', its decline and the need to restore its well-being. We then turn to the manifestation of sovereignism, looking at both its endogenous – *i.e.* the conditions and values needed to restore the welfare of the community – and exogenous features – *i.e.* how the people should be protected against external threats and intrusions.

RRPPs' economic populist sovereignism in five countries

All our parties of interest illustrate the mix of economic populism and sovereignism as a response to global challenges. First, their discourse aims to build a 'true' community of the people sharing a common economic destiny which is perceived as being under threat from national-corrupt / cosmopolitan / anti-national elites and outsiders.

Underlying economic populism

As often emphasized in the literature, a central populist claim by RRPPs is that the power of the people should be paramount. Populism is strongly emphasized by the French FN which claims to 'give France its freedom back and give the people a voice' (FN, 2012, 2017). The FN's idealized economic people refers to a broad coalition of socioeconomic groups of the 'majority common people' (*La France d'en-bas*). For the FN, the people's economic well-being is declining and the elites are responsible for this. The people share a common economic destiny which is betrayed by a 'globalist' ideology (FN, 2017). As Le Pen explains: 'We are a great people, a people that knows that it carries within itself the means of its freedom, the affirmation of its values, its greatness, its destiny (…) It is its will that will save us from the forces of decline' (Le Pen, 2017).

Economic populism is a prominent feature of the Italian League, which claims that the overall economic well-being of the Italian people is declining. During the 2018 elections, the leader of the League, Matteo Salvini declared: 'Millions of Italians have asked us to retake control of this country (…) and free it from the constraints and cages that have brought back hunger, precariousness and insecurity in Europe' (Salvini, 2018). For the League, the people's true interests have been betrayed by political elites and the 'European Union which is at the service of banks and international finance' (Lega, 2018). The Italian Lega's discourse typically stresses a Manichean vision of populism. As Salvini explains: 'Today it is no longer Right versus Left, but the People versus the Elite' (Cremonesi, 2018). 'I am and will always be proudly populist, Salvini said. People are fed up with the self-righteous radical chic people who despise the worker and never do their own shopping' (Salvini, 2018).

The FPÖ consistently emphasizes economic populism, stressing in particular the necessity to prioritize the benefits of the Austrian people's prosperity: 'Austria's prosperity, which has been hard earned over generations, must be secured for the future. It must be used primarily for such people and their descendants who have worked for it' (FPÖ, 2011). At the same time, the party criticizes bureaucracy, accused of limiting economic growth, and EU centralism which undermines national sovereignty (FPÖ, 2017).

Economic populist sovereigntist themes are given considerable attention in UKIP's program. These were central for instance to the 2015 campaign: 'We want Britain to be a free, independent, sovereign democracy' (UKIP, 2015). UKIP's populism has an economic connotation, opposing the true community of 'real people' to financial elites and the Westminster political establishment, while claiming to 'rebalance power from large corporations and big government institutions and put it back into the hands of the people of this country' (UKIP, 2015). UKIP also claims to 'speak up for the left out, those who work hard and play by the rules but have no special connections or market power', emphasizing in particular the role of 'small businesses' as the 'lifeblood of our economy' (UKIP, 2017). As Farage explains: 'Living standards have fallen and life has become a lot tougher for so many in our country. (…) The wellbeing of those living and working in our country matters to me more than GDP figures' (Farage, 2016).

Like UKIP, the SVP is mainly neo-liberal in its orientation (Mazzoleni & Rossini, 2014). The SVP has become radicalized under the leadership of Christoph Blocher, a multi-billionaire and businessman in industry and the financial sector. Under Blocher, economic populist and sovereigntist topics and issues have repeatedly been salient for the SVP, based on the underlying argument that what is good for the Swiss economy is also good for Swiss citizens (Blocher, 2016, pp. 14–15). The party advocates a Switzerland founded on a community of small and middle-class entrepreneurs and workers, which form the idealized populist coalition of the SVP. It is emphasized that this community is the real source of the country's wealth and economic well-being, which must be protected from threats, both domestic and international.

Targeting those who threaten national well-being, all these parties consistently highlight the 'national community' in terms of jobs and housing, while pledging to cut immigration and exclude the undeserving poor from the welfare state. Immigration is a crucial issue for the FN, for instance, which advocates drastically reducing immigration, which is seen as a burden for the country (FN, 2012, 2017). As Le Pen explains: 'We have nothing left to offer. We have seven million unemployed persons, we have nine million poor who should be the focus of all our energy' (cited in Gaveau, 2017). For the FN, 'outsiders' also include such undeserving poor as social fraudsters who should be excluded from welfare and punished (FN, 2012, 2017).

The League carries a strong anti-immigration message, accusing immigrants of stealing jobs from Italians and draining social welfare. Anti-immigration themes have been prioritized by the League under Salvini's leadership since 2014, unambiguously using nativist arguments such as 'stop the invasion' and 'Italians first' (*prima gli Italiani*) (Lega, 2017). As Salvini explained during the 2018 election campaign: 'I want to think first about those 5 million Italians in difficulty. I can't open my doors to the whole world.' Salvini also pledged that he would expel half a million illegal immigrants (Rainews, 2018).

Similarly, immigration is very prominent in UKIP's platforms, which consistently emphasize the need to reduce immigration to Britain. According to Farage, immigration is 'undercutting British workers' and 'damaging the lifestyle of millions of British families' (BBC, 2015). The 2015 manifesto pledged to 'put the "national" back into our national health service,' including a range of nativist policies such as 'limiting access to NHS and welfare for new migrants' (UKIP, 2015). Nativism was predominant in the 2017 platform, claiming for instance that 'British jobs should be offered first to British workers' (UKIP, 2017).

Opposition to 'mass immigration' is a salient issue in the Austrian FPÖ agenda, which not only emphasizes the 'risk of parallel societies' and the increasing presence of Islam, but also the threat of immigration for the labor market and state finances. The FPÖ refuses to accept new immigrants beyond those strictly needed in the labor market (Strache, 2017). Its 2017 electoral program sees 'mass immigration' (*Überfremdung*) as a 'huge business at the expense of Austrians' (FPÖ, 2017). Like the other parties in this study, the FPÖ strongly emphasizes the fight 'against social welfare abuse' while encouraging 'economic performance' (FPÖ, 2011, 2017).

Finally, turning to the Swiss case, mobilization against 'mass immigration' is a consistently salient issue for the SVP, similarly framed in terms of prosperity risks for Swiss citizens. As stated in the party's manifesto: 'Today's excessive immigration is jeopardising our freedom, our security, full employment, our landscape and, ultimately, our prosperity'

(SVP, 2015). The SVP sees immigration as having a wide-ranging negative impact on the country's well-being:

> increasing unemployment (…) overflowing trains, congested streets, rising rents and land prices, loss of valuable cultivated land as a result of building developments, wage pressure, a crowded labour market, cultural change in top management and a high percentage of foreigners burdening public welfare and other social institutions. (SVP, 2015)

Sovereignty claims

All five parties strongly emphasize sovereigntist discourse and frames. They all advocate popular power against political elites while also re-asserting the power of national authorities, their exclusive control over laws and international bodies, and consequently over the conditions under which the people's well-being should be safeguarded or restored.

Sovereignty is a crucial issue for the FN (Ivaldi, 2018). According to the 2017 platform: 'We will regain our freedom and control over our destiny by restoring the French people's sovereignty over their currency, borders, economy and laws' (FN, 2017). The exogenous component of FN sovereignism is primarily expressed in reaction to European integration, advocating for the EU to revert to a loose coalition of cooperating member states within a 'Europe of Nations' (FN, 2012, 2017). Both the 2012 and 2017 campaigns emphasized the need for a referendum on leaving the Eurozone as a means of restoring popular and national economic sovereignty (FN, 2012, 2017). The FN's sovereignism focuses on economic protectionism and strong criticism of supranational institutions and mechanisms, opposing free trade, large corporations and international financial institutions like the IMF and WTO (FN, 2012, 2017). Additionally, sovereignism is expressed in the area of foreign policy where the FN pledges to pull France out of NATO, while advocating closer relations with Russia. Moreover, the party pledges to 'renationalize the European Common Agricultural Policy (CAP)' to defend French farmers (FN, 2012, 2017). Regarding endogenous sovereignism, the FN advocates a Keynesian platform of redistribution, State interventionism (*dirigisme*) and public services, combined with tax cuts for small businesses (FN, 2012, 2017).

The Italian League also places popular and national sovereignty at the core of its political project, by 'putting Italian national interests first' (Lega, 2017, 2018). The League claims to defend the interests of the common people: its party manifesto calls for a 'common-sense revolution' (*Rivoluzione del buonsenso*) to 'give our children the certainty of a better future' (Lega, 2018). The endogenous component of sovereignism is expressed in La Lega's notions of locally entrenched capitalism and 'domestic production'. The party pledges to defend the interests of small businesses, reduce bureaucracy and cut corporate taxes, denouncing the 'thief state' (*stato ladro*), while also calling for a 'flat tax' for all Italian families (Lega, 2017, 2018). Externally, the League advocates 'restoring monetary, economic, territorial and legislative national sovereignty', reinforcing border control and repealing the Schengen Agreement (Lega, 2017, 2018). As stated in the 2018 manifesto: 'We must preserve our sovereignty, that is the right to be the masters of our own future and to protect ourselves from any foreign interference' (Lega, 2018). National courts should have supremacy over the European Court of Justice, and the EU should no longer have the power to conclude international agreements on behalf of Member States (Lega, 2018).

Pledges to put 'Austria first' are a consistently prominent feature of the FPÖ's party programs. Norbert Hofer, the FPÖ candidate for the 2016 presidential elections, clearly rejected the 'erosion of sovereignty by Brussels', arguing in favor of direct-democratic decisions as in Switzerland (NFZ, 2016). In a similar vein, the 2017 national election platform criticized the EU as a 'centralized, bureaucratized Moloch that threatens freedom' (FPÖ, 2017). Popular sovereigntist claims were toned down in the 2017 elections, but the party's platform continued to oppose international and multilateral trade agreements like TTIP and CETA, while claiming to 'stand for an EU as an association of independent countries and sovereign nations' (FPÖ, 2017). In the domestic realm, the FPÖ embraces tax relief for businesses and families, greatly reduced 'bureaucracy', as well as cuts in social expenditure, highlighting the role of small businesses in job creation and of farmers as 'guardians of the national culture' (FPÖ, 2017). The party consistently stresses its commitment to 'a market economy with social responsibility', promoting a 'focus on performance' to 'encourage a strong work ethic and facilitate ownership and prosperity' (FPÖ, 2011). The 2017 manifesto also reiterated its commitment to the national 'welfare state for Austrian citizens who have worked hard all their lives' (FPÖ, 2017).

The need to restore the national state in the interests of the British people can be seen as UKIP's political *raison d'être*. Externally, UKIP claims that British authorities should have exclusive control over laws and international interactions, rejecting external influence from the EU, depicted as a threat to national and popular sovereignty (UKIP, 2015, 2017). The 2015 manifesto wholeheartedly embraced Brexit as 'the only choice open to us, if we are to make our own laws and control our own destiny' (UKIP, 2015). Unlike the FN and the Italian League, however, UKIP's economic sovereignism is embedded in globalization, Atlanticism and free trade, with particular emphasis on ties with the 'Anglosphere' and NATO membership (UKIP, 2015, 2017). Scepticism towards international agreements is expressed mainly in the pledge to 'repeal the 2008 Climate Change Act' (UKIP, 2015, 2017). Regarding endogenous features, UKIP adopts a mixed economic platform, supporting small businesses and farmers, low taxation and increased spending on vital services like the NHS, while claiming to fight tax dodging by multinational corporations (UKIP, 2015, 2017).

Claims of national sovereignty are a predominant feature of the SVP. Externally, sovereignism is found primarily in the SVP's recurrent fight against a 'closer relationship between Switzerland and the EU', and its claim to protect national independence as a way of defending the country's well-being. As stated in the party's 2015 manifesto:

> Switzerland essentially owes its success to its special form of state embodying the pillars of independence, direct democracy, neutrality and federalism. (...) It was only thanks to these pillars of success that our country was able to achieve and maintain its place in the world as an economic leader, and it is only thanks to these pillars that freedom and welfare are preserved. (SVP, 2015, p. 8)

The EU is presented as a 'bureaucratic monster' undermining Swiss democracy and sovereignty: 'The sale of Swiss sovereignty and self-determination by the political elite must be stopped. Therefore, our country must no longer be insidiously integrated into international structures such as the EU' (SVP, 2015, p. 4). The endogenous component of the SVP's economic sovereignism is inspired by peasant tradition, liberal values and business ethics. According to the SVP, 'farmers are a key pillar of liberal thinking, corporate culture and family business, safeguarding our rural cultural heritage' (SVP, 2011, p. 66). The SVP prioritizes a less interventionist, more work-oriented and less bureaucratic state. The SVP's platform also stresses the 'Protestant work ethic' as the 'foundation for an entrepreneurial and performance-driven society' (SVP, 2015, p. 91), while opposing *Sozialliberalismus* and new-left culture which undermine duties over community and 'Switzerland as a workplace' (Hildebrand, 2017, pp. 181–182).

Discussion

The analysis in this paper corroborates that, while displaying discordant positions on traditional left-right economic issues, RRPPs show commonality on economic populism and sovereignism. Economic populist sovereignism forms a consistently salient and coherent set of issues for those parties. All five parties portray themselves as champions of national values and defenders of national interests against supranational institutions, most notably the EU, advocating the precedence of national legislation over international rules. They make claims of popular and national 'sovereignty' paramount in order to defend the people's self-identified economic interests and well-being. Thus, their 'people' is defined in economic, not only or not necessarily in cultural terms. As Mény and Surel (2000, p. 195) argue, the 'people' may also have an economic meaning as the 'people-class'. All the parties in this study see the 'true' community of people as sharing a common economic destiny, currently on the decline and under threat from such external forces as immigrants, cosmopolitan elites and international forces.

They all believe in the primacy of the nation-state as a means of re-establishing the people's sovereignty and economic well-being, although their sovereignism may refer to different economic prescriptions in domestic politics and different orientations in the area of trade and foreign economic relations. For instance, sovereignism for UKIP and the SVP fully embraces a free-trade agenda to bolster economic growth and national competitiveness, and these parties see economic openness as mostly beneficial to national prosperity. On the other hand, the FN, League and FPÖ see economic globalization mainly as a menace, and their sovereignism emphasizes protectionism as a means of defending national interests.

Looking at how the FN, SVP, FPÖ, League and UKIP define the 'economic' people, we see that these parties' discourses of economic sovereignism refer primarily to productive forces within the national community, which should be the 'true' beneficiaries of national wealth. The claim to represent the economic interests of the nation's 'producers' – *i.e.* the working and middle-class, as well as small entrepreneurs – against the elite, outsiders and large multinational corporations shares strong similarities with 'producerism' in the United States. Producerism is seen as a key feature of American right-wing populism, which postulates that hardworking people who create goods and wealth should be protected against 'parasites' at both the top and bottom of society (Berlet, 2012; Kazin, 1998).

In particular, we find commonality in economic policies directed at the economic groups that traditionally support such parties and which are seen as backbones of economic prosperity – that is, small businesses. All our parties regard small and medium-sized enterprises as an engine of economic development and job creation, making a valuable contribution to the nation's economic strength. They all embrace a typical right-wing pro-small business agenda of tax reduction and easing the bureaucratic burden on small entrepreneurs. Additionally, our RRPPs share a common agrarian appeal advocating selective agricultural protectionist policies and strong government action to protect the interests of farmers who are seen as another backbone of national economic prosperity as well as the typical possessors of values of national sovereignty and entrenchment.

Finally, all five parties share implicit 'nostalgia of the good old times' (Betz & Johnson, 2004, p. 324), where old times are defined not only as a period where 'real' values and identity prevailed, against multiculturalism, for instance, but also as a period of economic well-being represented by *Les Trente Glorieuses* – the 'Glorious Thirty' – from 1945 to 1975 in Western Europe. This sense of 'nostalgia' and its intersection with the promise of immediate unmediated policy changes link all the RRPPs in this study.

Conclusion

Departing from the literature on RRPP left-right economics, this article argues that the political economy of such parties is characterized primarily by economic populism and economic sovereignism, in relation with their populist and nationalist ideology. RRPPs prioritize the economic interests of the nation and the people, and the restoration of their well-being which, according to these parties, is on the decline. Their economic sovereignism emphasizes the need to 'regain control' on behalf of the community as a means of restoring its well-being. Economic sovereigntist claims, both endogenous – *e.g.* welfare chauvinism and producerism – and exogenous – *e.g.* economic protectionism and free-tradism – take on different forms across parties and contexts by mixing different economic policy orientations at both the national and supranational level.

Moreover, economic sovereignism may be seen as the way in which economic populism expresses its 'redemptive' component. By focusing on economic sovereignism, this paper suggests that the 'redemptive' face of populism – *i.e.* the promise of salvation by re-empowering the people (Canovan, 1999) and the sovereigntist orientation of right-wing populist 'dislocation' (Laclau, 2005) – should be made more central to our understanding of the political economy of right-wing populism. As a project for immediate renewal and economic prosperity, however, right-wing populism often celebrates an imaginary 'heartland' (Taggart, 2000) inspired by an idealized economic past, something to return to. In that sense, economic populism can be seen as a counter-utopian project, a 'eutopia' that is both possible and actionable (Kallis, 2018, p. 286).

In our view, the supply-side approach to RRPP political economy developed in this paper has significant implications for our general understanding of populist radical right-wing mobilization. First, this paper consolidates the current literature that argues that RRPP economics are best captured by such parties' core populist radical-right ideology, less so by traditional left-right economic issues. While scholars often discuss the 'inconsistency' and variability of RRPP economics, we find, on the contrary, that such parties produce a consistently coherent economic policy program. Despite diverging economic policy prescriptions, Europe's main RRPPs share a common frame that emphasizes economic populism combined with claims of sovereignty.

While our empirical analysis remains primarily descriptive, our findings provide suggestions for future research which should pay more attention to the factors underlying variation in economic populism and sovereignism by RRPPs. Differences should be addressed in relation to intra-party dynamics and party leadership and the opportunity structures in which such parties function and compete. The economic, cultural and political competition associated with the 'denationalization' process is putting increasing strain on the national political community (Kriesi et al., 2008), resulting in the crystallization of 'transnational' conflict which provides new political opportunities for RRPPs (Hooghe & Marks, 2018). At the same time, the dominant norms and values of national economic cultures and models of capitalism (*e.g.* Bornschier, 2005; Esping-Andersen, 1990), as well as external shocks like the global economic crisis, may provide different contexts, resources and incentives for economic populist sovereignism, regarding variation in their economically protectionist agendas in particular.

Our findings may also foster future research on how the typical 'economic populist sovereignism' identified in this paper may circulate across regions and also penetrate mainstream politics. We should ask, for instance, whether populist sovereigntist frames are found in regions with different political economy cultures as in Eastern and Central Europe, where successful right-wing populist players like Viktor Orban's Fidesz in Hungary and Poland's Law and Justice Party (PiS) may produce their own idiosyncrasy in terms of economic populist sovereignism. We should also look into the overall impact of economic populist sovereignism on mainstream parties. The political rise of Trumpism in the USA illustrates the importance of populist, sovereigntist and producerist features in the recent transformation of the Republican Party. As illustrated with the current Brexit crisis and populist governments in the United States and Italy, claims of national sovereignty are moving increasingly into mainstream politics under populist pressure, and this may deeply affect economic policies and international trade relations in the future.

Finally, our paper may inform future research on other party families, as economic populism and sovereignism may be observed across a variety of political players, in articulation with other sets of beliefs and values (Kallis, 2018). For instance, the mix of economic populism and sovereignism has recently materialized in left-wing populist parties like La France Insoumise (LFI) in France (Ivaldi, 2018) and Podemos in Spain, as well as in new populist idiosyncrasies outside the traditional left-right spectrum, like the Movimento 5 Stelle (M5S) in Italy (Gerbaudo & Screti, 2017; Ivaldi, Lanzone, & Woods, 2017; Vittori, 2017). As a response to globalization pressure and 'loss of sovereignty', the mix of economic populism and sovereignism may increasingly form a successful mobilization frame available to a wider range of populist parties and entrepreneurs across established democracies around the world.

ORCID

Gilles Ivaldi ⓘ http://orcid.org/0000-0001-5849-1138
Oscar Mazzoleni ⓘ http://orcid.org/0000-0002-2535-613X

References

Afonso, A., & Rennwald, L. (2018). Social class and the changing welfare state agenda of radical right parties in Europe. In P. Manow, C. Palier, & H. Schwander (Eds.), *Welfare democracies and party politics* (pp. 171–196). Oxford: Oxford University Press.

Akkerman, A., Zaslove, A., & Spruyt, B. (2017). 'We the people' or 'we the peoples'? A comparison of support for the populist radical right and populist radical left in the Netherlands. *Swiss Political Science Review*, *23*(4), 377–403.

BBC. (2015). *UKIP's Farage wants 50,000-a-year cap on migrants*. April 2, 2015, Retrieved from https://www.bbc.com/news/election-2015-32160667.

Benford, R. D., & Snow, D. A. (2000). Framing processes and social movements: An overview and assessment. *Annual Review of Sociology*, *26*, 611–639.

Berlet, C. (2012). Reframing populist resentments in the tea party movement. In L. Rosenthal, & C. Trost (Eds.), *Steep. The Precipitous rise of the Tea party* (pp. 47–66). Berkeley: California University Press.

Betz, H. G. (1994). *Radical right-wing populism in Western Europe*. London: Palgrave Macmillan.

Betz, H. G., & Johnson, C. (2004). Against the current — stemming the tide: The nostalgic ideology of the contemporary radical populist right. *Journal of Political Ideologies*, *9*(3), 311–327.

Betz, H.-G., & Meret, S. (2013). Right-wing populist parties and the working-class vote: What have you done for us lately? In J. Rydgren (Ed.), *Class politics and the radical right* (pp. 107–121). London: Routledge.

Blocher, C. (2016). *La Suisse sur la voie vers la dictature. Discours de l'Albisgüetli, Meeting of the Zurich SVP*. January 15.

Bornschier, V. (2005). *Culture and politics in economic development*. New York: Routledge.

Canovan, M. (1999). Trust the people! populism and the two faces of democracy. *Political Studies*, *47*(1), 2–16.

Canovan, M. (2005). *The people*. Cambridge: Polity Press.

Chryssogelos, A. (2018). State transformation and populism: From the internationalized to the neo-sovereign state? *Politics*. https://doi.org/10.1177%2F0263395718803830. on-line first.

Cremonesi, M. (2018). Salvini liquida il centrodestra: la prospettiva è popolo contro élite. *Corriere della Sera*, May 22, 2018. Retrieved from https://milano.corriere.it/notizie/politica/18_maggio_22/salvini-liquida-centrodestra-prospettiva-popolo-contro-elite-bc228452-5d80-11e8-b13c-dd6bf73f9db5.shtml.

De Cleen, B., & Stavrakakis, Y. (2017). Distinctions and articulations: A discourse theoretical framework for the study of populism and nationalism. *Javnost - The Public*, *24*(4), 301–319.

De Lange, S. L. (2007). A new winning formula? The programmatic appeal of the radical right. *Party Politics*, *13*(4), 411–435.

De Spiegeleire, S., Skinner, C., & Sweijs, T. (2017). *The rise of populist sovereigntism: What it is, where it comes from, and what it means for international security and Defense*. The Hague: Centre for Strategic Studies.

Eger, A. M., & Valdez, S. (2015). Neo-nationalism in Western Europe. *European Sociological Review*, *31*(1), 115–130.

Ennser-Jedenastik, L. (2016). A welfare state for whom? A group-based account of the Austrian freedom party's social policy profile. *Swiss Political Science Review*, *22*(3), 409–427.

Esping-Andersen, G. (1990). *The three worlds of welfare capitalism*. Cambridge: Polity Press.

Farage, N. (2016). Why we must vote LEAVE in the EU referendum. *Express*, June 21, 2016. Retrieved from https://www.express.co.uk/comment/expresscomment/681776/nigel-farage-eu-referendum-brexit-vote-leave-independence-ukip.

Ford, R., & Goodwin, M. (2014). *Revolt on the right: Explaining support for the radical right in Britain*. London: Routledge.

Gaveau, C. (2017). *Le Grand Débat: Marine Le Pen veut arrêter l'immigration légale et illégale, RTL*, March 21, 2017. Retrieved from http://www.rtl.fr/actu/politique/le-grand-debat-marine-le-pen-veut-arreter-l-immigration-legale-et-illegale-7787750935.

Gerbaudo, P., & Screti, F. (2017). Reclaiming popular sovereignty: The vision of the state in the discourse of Podemos and the Movimento 5 Stelle. *Javnost - The Public*, *24*(4), 320–335.

Harteveld, E. (2016). Winning the 'losers' but losing the 'winners'. The electoral consequences of the radical right moving to the economic left. *Electoral Studies*, *44*, 225–234.

Heinisch, R., Holtz-Bacha, C., & Mazzoleni, O. (Eds.). (2017). *Political populism. A handbook*. Baden-Baden: Nomos.

Hermet, G. (2001). *Les populismes dans le monde. Une histoire sociologique, 19e-20e siècle.* Paris: Fayard.

Hildebrand, M. (2017). *Rechtspopulismus und Hegemonie: Der Aufstieg der SVP und die diskursive Transformation der politischen Schweiz.* Bielefeld: Transcript.

Ivaldi, G. (2018). Contesting the EU in times of crises: The front national and politics of Euroscepticism in France. *Politics*, Online first, https://doi.org/10.1177/0263395718766787.

Ivaldi, G., Lanzone, M. E., & Woods, D. (2017). Varieties of populism across a left-right spectrum: The case of the front national, the Northern league, Podemos and five star movement. *Swiss Political Science Review, 23*(4), 354–376.

Kallis, A. (2018). Populism, sovereigntism, and the unlikely re-emergence of the territorial nation-state. *Fudan Journal of the Humanities and Social Sciences, 11*(3), 285–302.

Kazin, M. (1998). *The populist persuasion.* Ithaca & London: Cornell University Press.

Kitschelt, H., & McGann, A. J. (1995). *The radical right in Western Europe. A comparative analysis.* Ann Arbor: Michigan University Press.

Kriesi, H.-P., Grande, E., Lachat, R., Dolezal, M., Bornschier, S., & Frey, T. (2008). *West European politics in the age of globalization.* Cambridge: Cambridge University Press.

Lacewell, O. P. (2017). Beyond policy positions: How party type conditions programmatic responses to globalization pressures. *Party Politics, 23*(4), 448–460.

Laclau, E. (2005). *On populist reason.* London & New York: Verso.

Lefkofridi, Z., & Michel, E. (2014). The electoral politics of solidarity. The welfare state agendas of radical right. In K. Banting, & W. Kymlicka (Eds.), *The strains of commitment. The political sources of solidarity in diverse societies* (pp. 233–267). Oxford: Oxford University Press.

Le Pen, M. (2017). *Assises présidentielles de Lyon: Discours de Marine Le Pen.* February 5, 2017. Retrieved from http://www.frontnational.com/videos/assises-presidentielles-de-lyon-discours-de-marine-le-pen/.

Liesbet, H., & Gary, Marks. (2018). Cleavage theory meets Europe's crises: Lipset, Rokkan, and the transnational cleavage. *Journal of European Public Policy, 25*(1), 109–135.

Marks, G. (2007). Special symposium: Comparing measures of party positioning: Expert, manifesto, and survey data. *Electoral Studies, 26*(1), 1–10.

Mazzoleni, O., & Rossini, C. (2014). Salience, orientation and content of socio-economic issues: the electoral manifesto of the Swiss People's Party (1995–2011). Paper presented at the ECPR General Conference, Glasgow, 3-6 September.

Mény, Y., & Surel, Y. (2000). *Par le Peuple, Pour le Peuple. Le Populisme et la Démocratie.* Paris: Fayard.

Mudde, C. (2007). *Populist radical right parties in Europe.* Cambridge: Cambridge University Press.

Mudde, C. (2016). *The study of populist radical right parties: Towards a fourth wave.* C-REX Working Paper Series, no. 1. Oslo: University of Oslo.

Mudde, C., & Rovira Kaltwasser, C. (2013). Exclusionary vs. inclusionary populism: Comparing contemporary Europe and Latin America. *Government and Opposition, 48*(2), 147–174.

Otjes, S., Ivaldi, G., Ravik Jupskås, A., & Mazzoleni, O. (2018). It's not economic interventionism, stupid! Reassessing the political economy of radical right-wing populist parties. *Swiss Political Science Review, 24*(3), 270–290.

Rainews. (2018). *In Italia ci sono troppi clandestini che vanno in giro a fare casino.* January 23, 2018. Retrieved from http://www.rainews.it/dl/rainews/articoli/Salvini-come-Trump-Lo-slogan-prima-gli-italiani-bec239ea-66ec-4fc7-9f01-44dbfe6160b4.html.

Rovira Kaltwasser, C., Taggart, P., Espejoaulina, O. P., & Ostigu, P. (Eds.). (2017). *The Oxford Handbook of populism.* Oxford: OUP.

Salvini, M. (2018). *Salvini: 'Sono e sarò sempre orgogliosamente populista.* March 5, 2018. Retrieved from https://www.youtube.com/watch?v=wBTbN8yrFMQ.

Sassen, S. (2015). *Losing control? Sovereignty in an age of globalization.* New York: Columbia University Press.

Seawright, J., & Gerring, J. (2008). Case selection techniques in case study research: A menu of qualitative and quantitative Options. *Political Research Quarterly, 61*(2), 294–308.

Strache. (2017). HC Strache: Wir wollen illegale Migration stoppen. *FPÖ TV*, November 17, 2017. Retrieved from https://www.youtube.com/watch?v=m7WpPdrWtYg.

Taggart, P. (2000). *Populism.* Buckingham: Open University Press.

Urbinati, N. (2014). *Democracy disfigured. Opinion, truth, and the people.* Cambridge: Harvard University Press.

Van der Brug, W., & Van Spanje, J. (2009). Immigration, Europe and the 'new' cultural dimension. *European Journal of Political Research*, 48(3), 309–334.

Vittori, D. (2017). Podemos and the five-star movement: Populist, nationalist or what? *Contemporary Italian Politics*, 9(2), 142–161.

Zaslove, A. (2008). Exclusion, community and a populist political economy: The radical right as an anti-globalization movement. *Comparative European Politics*, 6(2), 169–189.

Appendix A. List of Party Manifestos considered in the analysis

---

FN (2012) *Mon Projet pour la France et les Français. Marine Le Pen, la Voix du Peuple, l'Esprit de la France*. Retrieved from: https://archive.org/details/EL245_P_2012_120/page/n15

FN (2017). *144 Engagements présidentiels, Marine 2017*. Retrieved from: https://rassemblementnational.fr/le-projet-de-marine-le-pen/

FPÖ (2011). *Parteiprogramm der Freiheitlichen Partei Österreichs, 18. Juni 2011* (retrieved from: https://www.fpoe.at/themen/parteiprogramm).

NFZ (2016), Hofer ist Kontrapunkt zu 'Einheitskandidaten', *Neue Freie Zeitung*, 10.3.2016 (retrieved from: https://www.fpoe.at/artikel/hofer-ist-kontrapunkt-zu-einheitskandidaten/)

FPÖ (2017). *Österreicher verdienen Fairness. Freiheitliches Wahlprogramm zur Nationalratswahl 2017*. Retrieved from: https://www.fpoe.at/fileadmin/user_upload/Wahlprogramm_8_9_low.pdf

SVP (2011). *SVP – The Party for Switzerland. Party Programme of the Swiss People's Party 2011–2015*. Bern. Retrieved from https://www.svp.ch

SVP (2015). *SVP – The Party for Switzerland. Party Programme of the Swiss People's Party 2015–2019*. Bern. Retrieved from https://www.svp.ch

UKIP (2015). *Believe in Britain. UKIP 2015 Manifesto*. Retrieved from: https://d3n8a8pro7vhmx.cloudfront.net/ukipdev/pages/1103/attachments/original/1429295050/UKIPManifesto2015.pdf

UKIP (2017). *Britain together. UKIP 2017 Manifesto*. Retrieved from: https://d3n8a8pro7vhmx.cloudfront.net/ukipdev/pages/3944/attachments/original/1495695469/UKIP_Manifesto_June2017opt.pdf?1495695469

UKIP (2018). *About UKIP.* (Retrieved 8 from http://www.ukip.org/about)

Lega (2018). *Elezioni 2018. Programma di Governo. Salvini Premier: La R. del Buonsenso*. Retrieved from: https://www.leganord.org/programma-politiche

---

Appendix B. List of additional documents considered in the analysis

BBC. (2015). *UKIP's Farage wants 50,000-a-year cap on migrants.* April 2, 2015, Retrieved from https://www.bbc.com/news/election-2015-32160667

Blocher, C. (2016). *La Suisse sur la voie vers la dictature. Discours de l'Albisgüetli, Meeting of the Zurich SVP.* January 15.

Cremonesi, M. (2018). Salvini liquida il centrodestra: la prospettiva è popolo contro élite. *Corriere della Sera*, May 22, 2018. Retrieved from https://milano.corriere.it/notizie/politica/18_maggio_22/salvini-liquida-centrodestra-prospettiva-popolo-contro-elite-bc228452-5d80-11e8-b13c-dd6bf73f9db5.shtml

Farage, N. (2016). Why we must vote LEAVE in the EU referendum. *Express*, June 21, 2016. Retrieved from https://www.express.co.uk/comment/expresscomment/681776/nigel-farage-eu-referendum-brexit-vote-leave-independence-ukip

Gaveau, C. (2017). *Le Grand Débat: Marine Le Pen veut arrêter l'immigration légale et illégale, RTL*, March 21, 2017. Retrieved from http://www.rtl.fr/actu/politique/le-grand-debat-marine-le-pen-veut-arreter-l-immigration-legale-et-illegale-7787750935

Le Pen, M. (2017). *Assises présidentielles de Lyon: Discours de Marine Le Pen*. February 5, 2017. Retrieved from http://www.frontnational.com/videos/assises-presidentielles-de-lyon-discours-de-marine-le-pen/

Rainews. (2018). *In Italia ci sono troppi clandestini che vanno in giro a fare casino.* January 23, 2018. Retrieved from http://www.rainews.it/dl/rainews/articoli/Salvini-come-Trump-Lo-slogan-prima-gli-italiani-bec239ea-66ec-4fc7-9f01-44dbfe6160b4.html

Salvini, M. (2018). *Salvini: 'Sono e sarò sempre orgogliosamente populista*. March 5, 2018. Retrieved from https://www.youtube.com/watch?v=wBTbN8yrFMQ

Strache. (2017). HC Strache: Wir wollen illegale Migration stoppen. *FPÖ TV*, November 17, 2017. Retrieved from https://www.youtube.com/watch?v=m7WpPdrWtYg

Taking back control? Brexit, sovereignism and populism in Westminster (2015–17)

Gianfranco Baldini, Edoardo Bressanelli and Stella Gianfreda

ABSTRACT
This article analyses the claims for national sovereignty made in the British Conservative and Labour parties. In Britain, national sovereignism has been embedded within an entrenched tradition of Euroscepticism, whereas populist claims have periodically punctuated the discourse of both main parties, before emerging with more vocal tones during the discussion on Brexit. While most sovereigntist claims share some degree of populism, we reserve the populist label for what we identify as explicitly populist claims (as opposed to four other categories of sovereignism). After presenting a historical recall of the main dynamics of sovereigntist claims in British politics, we hypothesise that different types of sovereigntist discourses feature in the major British parties. While 'nationalist-populist' sovereignism should prevail in the Conservative party, we expect 'economic' sovereignism to be the form mainly used by the Labour party. Systematically analysing the debates in the House of Commons on all divisions on the EU from the 2015 General Election to the end of October 2017, we show that significant differences on the use of sovereignist claims exist both within and across British parties. We find that national populist claims dominate among Tory MPs and civic sovereignism prevails over economic sovereignism among Labour members.

1. Introduction

Brexit stands out as an exemplar case for the reclaiming of national sovereignty by a country, the United Kingdom – 'the awkward partner' in Europe (George, 1998) – that has never been entirely comfortable with its membership of European institutions. The June 2016 referendum on EU membership did not come out of the blue. In an attempt to preserve some aspects of political and economic sovereignty, Britain had for many years acquired opt-outs in key areas (e.g. in terms of Economic and Monetary Union, and the Schengen Agreement), becoming the least integrated country in the context of an increasingly 'differentiated Europe' (Leuffen, Rittberger, & Schimmelfennig, 2012).

The predominant British view on how Europe should work was expressed by Margaret Thatcher in her famous Bruges speech in 1988, under the expression of 'willing cooperation between sovereign states'.

The idea that sovereignty should be retained by the member states was always particularly important for Britain, which had traditionally been governed by the principle of the 'absolute sovereignty' of the Westminster parliament. True, political sovereignty had been (at least partly) ceded by joining what was then the European Economic Community, in 1973. When Britain entered, Europe already had a new legal order (Bogdanor, 2016), as set in stone by key sentences of the European Court of Justice in the 1960s. But many politicians pretended to ignore that this was the case, and the people were barely interested in such 'technical' aspects (Saunders, 2018). Similarly, Britain hold its first state-wide referendum ever on Europe in 1975, and this was on the confirmation of the terms of the membership, rather than on the idea of joining – as happened in 1972 in the other countries that were part of the first enlargement in 1973, namely Ireland and Denmark (Norway also voted, but decided to stay out). As would soon become apparent, Britain's entry into Europe could not easily dispose of several historical, geographical and political peculiarities, which would be reinforced as integration proceeded (Gamble, 2003; Gifford, 2014; Grant, 2008).

Fast forward to 2016, and 'taking back control' was, together with the post-referendum idea of the 'will of the people', one of the key slogans of Brexit, which is in itself considered a key signing post for the emergence of a 'populist moment' in Western societies (Brubaker, 2017). To be sure, Britain has certainly seen the outburst of populist discourses in the past – especially with controversial politicians such as Enoch Powell (Sandbrook, 2018). Nevertheless, Brexit marks a shift in the importance of both populism and sovereignism, in a context in which the

> hardening of the "zero-sum" perspective on sovereignty that has been the node of contemporary populist discourses across the world underlines the necessity of not just arresting the process of transfer of power away from the territorial state but of reversing the flow altogether. (Kallis, 2018, p. 294)

A rich literature has analysed important claims for sovereignty that emerged during the referendum campaign (Curtice, 2017; Hobolt, 2016; Jackson, Thorsen, & Wring, 2016), with the principal aim of regaining control of the borders and retaining economic resources for domestic use. Other studies have looked at the populist rhetoric of Nigel Farage, one of the 'champions' of Brexit (Crines & Heppell, 2017; Pareschi & Albertini, 2018). In analysing the 2010–15 legislature, it has been argued that 'in championing popular sovereignty as expressed via a referendum, the Conservatives contributed to a populist critique that implicitly contrasted "cosmopolitan and political elites" with the "pure People"' (Wellings & Vines, 2016, p. 318). Our focus, therefore, is on the extent to which sovereigntist claims can also be considered populist: how are populist arguments related to the idea of taking back control? Can we detect any important trends within and across parties when comparing the pre- and the post-referendum phase?

Recent works have analysed the transformation of the Conservative party after the Brexit referendum (Lynch & Whitaker, 2018) and Labour's parliamentary patterns with regard to Corbyn's leadership (Crines, Jeffery, & Heppell, 2018), but we are not aware of any analysis that has considered the discourses of both parties in comparison. This is what we do in this article, by looking at how their sovereigntist and populist claims have unfolded during the Brexit process (2015–17).

In the rest of this article, we start (Section 2) from a definition of sovereignism and presenting a historical recall of the main dynamics of sovereignist claims in British politics. Section 3 then formulates expectations on the importance of sovereignism and populism in the Conservative Party and the Labour Party. Section 4 introduces the analysis of the parliamentary speeches in the House of Commons (2015–17), while Section 5 develops the empirical analysis. Finally, the article reflects more broadly on sovereignism, the EU and British party politics.

2. Reclaiming sovereignty in the motherland of Euroscepticism

Sovereignism can generally be understood as a response to economic, political and cultural competition triggered by globalisation. There are three processes that are likely to originate sovereignist claims: (a) increasing *economic competition* due to the internationalisation of trade and finance and the consequent growth of interdependence between national economies, (b) a (perceived) *cultural competition* brought about by the unprecedented mobility of different ethnic groups, largely favoured by technological developments and worldwide interconnectedness, and (c) a *political competition* between nation-states and supra- or international institutions and technocratic bodies for the control of the decision-making process of an increasing number of policy areas (Kriesi et al., 2012; Kriesi et al., 2008). In Britain, however, sovereignism strongly overlaps with Euroscepticism, with sovereignist claims often made in opposition to EU membership. While all the sovereignist claims share some populist traits in reclaiming power to the country, we prefer to reserve the populist label for claims that more directly and explicitly invoke power to the people as against the alleged usurpation of power from the political elites. Following the multidimensional conceptualisation of sovereignism proposed by Basile and Mazzoleni (2020), we conceptualise it as follows:

(1) *Economic*: opposition towards the EU's economic governance, namely, the European Economic and Monetary Union.
(2) *National*: opposition towards the process of political integration or EU-deepening, namely the transfer to European institutions of decision-making powers in an increasing number of policy areas.
(3) *Populist*: opposition towards European elites and institutions, particularly their lack of legitimacy and accountability vis-à-vis the 'will of the people'.
(4) *Civic*: opposition to the effects of European integration on the mechanisms of representative democracy, particularly on the centrality of national parliaments.
(5) *Cultural:* opposition to the cultural effects of European integration on domestic society and culture, particularly on social cohesion and internal security.

Populism, according to a now classic definition (Mudde, 2007, p. 23), is a thin ideology that opposes 'the corrupt elites' (in our case, the EU 'technocrats' and 'bureaucrats') to 'the pure people'. While we share some of the criticisms raised by Heinisch and Mazzoleni (2017) on some limitations of the ideational approach as popularised by Mudde, we consider the Manichean juxtaposition between people and elite as defined by Mudde a key reference point for our analysis of parliamentary speeches (as does most research on this topic: see Aslanidis, 2018). In this respect, populism clearly is an instance of sovereignism, by advocating 'bringing back control' as unresponsive supranational elites disregard the will of the (British) people. On the other hand, however, sovereignism can take different forms and its populist facet does not need to be dominant, nor even prevalent (cf. Basile & Mazzoleni, 2020, p. 5).

Tracing back in time the emergence of sovereignist discourses and opposition to the EU project, a rich body of literature has shown that the approval of the Maastricht treaty in 1992 was a turning point for the emergence of lukewarm or hostile sentiments, setting the stage for the shift from 'permissive consensus' to 'constraining dissensus' in many member states (Hooghe & Marks, 2012). However, Britain had been at odds with some aspects of the European project long before Maastricht. Indeed, Europe has been a divisive issue inside the Westminster parliament even before the country joined the then European Economic Community (EEC) in 1973 (Norton, 1980). The United Kingdom is not just the motherland of representative government (Judge, 2005), but also the country where hostility to Europe has divided both main parties, first bringing about the split of the Social Democratic Party from Labour in 1981, then being a decisive factor in the long journey back to power for the Conservatives (after 13 years of opposition between 1997 and 2010). But how was sovereignty related to the emergence of the hostility vis-à-vis Europe, which would ultimately lead to Brexit?

If the term Euroscepticism was first used by the newspaper *The Times* in 1985, the roots of British claims for sovereignty go much deeper than that (Menon & Salter, 2016). In Britain, furthermore, Euroscepticism has been also a mainstream phenomenon, as well as being (more recently) an anti-establishment element for challenger populist forces (as in all other West European countries). In Britain the term captured the hostility – framed by Margaret Thatcher in her Bruges speech of 1988 – to the further pooling of sovereignty and the birth of Economic and Monetary Union, two key elements in Europe in the decades that followed. Since then, albeit from different perspectives, both the Conservatives and the Labour Party (with the partial exceptions of the Blair and Brown premierships) have been in trouble in accepting the evolving architecture of the EU. At the same time, and again in a very peculiar way, the recent evolutions of the two parties mean that they cultivate very different conceptions of sovereignty, and therefore also very different forms of Euroscepticism (see further in Section 3).

Claims for national sovereignty have always been important in post-war British history, and we can find key examples of them in all the five dimensions that we then analyse in the rest of the paper. Back in 1962, the Labour leader Hugh Gaitskell spoke against the possible emergence of the United States of Europe, which would mean, 'the end of Britain as an independent nation state [...] of a thousand years of history'. Although mild, this was clearly a national-sovereignist claim, of which the most radical example would come in 1968, with Enoch Powell's famous 'river of blood speech', which had an anti-immigrant position of national sovereignty. Despite being condemned by the party, the speech was – according to some experts – an important factor in Edward Heath's Conservative victory of 1970. In 1992, the traumatic exit from the Exchange Rate Mechanism and the opposition to Maastricht in the following years were key expressions of claims of economic sovereignty. More recently, populist and national sovereignist claims have come together with the rise of migration as the most salient electoral issue (2010–15). In 2016, the supporters of 'Leave' in the EU referendum adopted 'Take back control' as their slogan, a paradigmatic case of a 'claim for national sovereignty'. A further sovereigntist claim has a civic element and is linked to the importance of British values and institutions. As Vivien A. Schmidt puts it:

> Sovereignty, rather than being associated solely with the executive as the embodiment of the state, as in France, was vested in the duality of the 'Crown in Parliament', constituting a sovereignty shared between the executive and the legislature. This ensured that any increase in the power of EU institutions would therefore be seen as a threat not just to executive autonomy but also to parliamentary sovereignty (2006, p. 28).

The intra-party divisiveness of sovereignism – intended here as opposition to EU integration – is evident by observing the voting behaviour of the two main parties in the House of Commons. From the 2015 General Election to the second reading of the EU Withdrawal Bill in October 2017, there have been 55 divisions on EU matters in the Commons: 19 in the 2015–16 session, 31 in the 2016–17 session, and 5 after the 2017 General Election and up to the end of October 2017. In the final year of David Cameron's premiership, the most divisive bill – an amendment to the EU Referendum Bill – counted 37 Tory rebels. In the Labour Party, the most rebels (10 MPs) were found on a vote to extend the voting rights in the EU referendum to EU citizens. Under the leadership of Theresa May, the most rebellious vote on the EU was on an amendment to the EU (Notification of Withdrawal) Bill, when 7 MPs voted against the government. On the third reading of the same bill, 52 Labour MPs defied the party whip.

To put the above rebellions in context, it is useful to compare them with the rebellions faced by the Conservatives and the Labour Party in the votes on the ratification of Maastricht and the Lisbon Treaty (Table 1). Of course, the comparison is not made between homogenous units: while the votes on Maastricht and the Lisbon Treaty were on the ratification of the Treaties, the three most important Bills on the EU in the 2015–17 period were on the EU referendum, on the notification of withdrawal (i.e. the triggering of Article 50 to start the withdrawal process), and on the withdrawal from the EU (i.e. repealing EU legislation and transposing it into British law). With this caveat in mind, the divisions on the implementation of the Treaty of Lisbon featured at most 20 Tory and 28 Labour rebels. The rebellions in the tumultuous votes on the Treaty of Maastricht were significantly larger – with a peak of 41 MPs voting against the Tory whip and 71 against the Labour

Table 1. Largest revolts on the EU in the major British parties from Maastricht to Brexit.

	Conservative Party	Labour Party
Maastricht *EC Amendment Bill*	41 (12.2 per cent)	71 (26.2 per cent)
Lisbon *EU Amendment Bill*	20 (10.1 per cent)	28 (7.9 per cent)

'Brexit' Bills
  EU Referendum Bill
  Notification of Withdrawal Bill
  EU Withdrawal Bill (2nd reading)
	37 (11.2 per cent)	52 (19.5 per cent)

Sources: Cowley & Norton, 1999; Cowley & Stuart, 2010; Hansard (various).
Notes: figures are the number and the share of rebel MPs.

leadership (the latter divided between 66 MPs opposing and 5 supporting the third reading of the Maastricht Bill).

In the aftermath of Brexit, the largest Tory rebellion so far occurred on the EU Referendum Bill, when 37 MPs voted with the Opposition and defeated Cameron's government. However, rebellions at the voting stage on other bills have been very limited, even in comparison with the ratification of the Treaty of Lisbon. For the Labour Party, on the other hand, the real troubles were to be found with regard to the Notification of Withdrawal Bill. In the 21 divisions on this bill, the Labour party split in all votes except one. Not only did 52 MPs vote against the whip at third reading, but 47 also voted against the bill at second reading, and 40 backed an amendment opposed by the leadership.

Interestingly, in the period after the referendum to October 2017 it is the Labour party that has suffered the most from its internal tensions on the EU. The Tories – both before and, for the time being, after the 2017 general elections – have been rather cohesive at least so far as their parliamentary votes are considered. It is clearly more important for the governing party to keep its unity, as splits inside the opposition parties are often inconsequential. Yet voting cohesion does not necessarily mean party unity. Significant differences within the Tory ranks clearly emerge when their parliamentary speeches, rather their parliamentary votes, are analysed – and may at some point be reflected in voting behaviour (see Section 5).

3. Hardening sovereignism at the core of the British party system

In Britain, the solidity of the party system has traditionally been embedded with the Westminster model, built on majoritarian institutions, the 'absolute sovereignty' of parliament, and especially on the enduring first-past-the-post electoral system, which – in normal times – fabricates a two-party system and cohesive single-party cabinets (cf. Baldini, Bressanelli, & Massetti, 2018). For a long time, this meant that the possible insurgence of fringe and anti-establishment parties was kept at bay, until the rise of Euroscepticism and the (late) adoption of a proportional system for the election of the European Parliament in 1999 allowed the emergence of the United Kingdom Independence Party (UKIP).

In 1997, when Blair became Prime Minister, the salience of Europe among public opinion reached its peak and a brand-new party like the Referendum Party got three per cent of the vote in the 1997 General Election – a result which would look rather meagre for a Eurosceptic party today, but which was at the time far from irrelevant. Incidentally, UKIP went on to build its rise on this result, by gaining one position – from fourth to first place – at each and every European Parliament election from 1999 to 2014, quadrupling its score from 6.6–26.6 per cent.

In the mid-2000s, the salience of Europe among British voters was back to the irrelevance experienced during the 1980s, and it would remain at this level until 2015 (Grande & Schwarzbözl, 2017, p. 31). It is in the run-up to the 2015 General Election that immigration became the most relevant issue in public opinion. While the EU as such was still not so salient, the (lack of) control on immigration was mainly framed as a consequence of the EU's freedom of movement. All parties embraced more restrictive positions on immigration, and David Cameron pledged to reduce net migration to under 100,000 entries per year. In 2015, UKIP won its first (and, so far, only) seat at Westminster, having already won two by-elections in the previous year. The first-past-the-post electoral system no longer appeared able to contain the success of challenger parties and the possibility of a referendum on the EU was looming larger and larger on British politics. With UKIP becoming a credible electoral threat, the Tories hardened their position on both immigration and European integration (Bale, 2018; Heppell, Crines, & Jeffery, 2017) with the pledge for a referendum on membership finally being made in the 2015 manifesto.

Although Cameron was still able to campaign for 'Remain' in the run-up to the referendum, and even if the Conservatives (or a section of the party) may still officially endorse a hyper-globalist position in economic terms (Baker, Gamble, & Seawright, 2002) – e.g. the 'global power' discourse articulated by Theresa May in several important speeches, such as, for instance, at Lancaster House ('I want us to be a truly Global Britain – the best friend and neighbour to our European partners, but a country that reaches beyond the borders of Europe too') – it is in the Conservative Party that nationalist and populist forms of sovereignism – what Freeden defined as 'national-populist' rhetoric (2017, pp. 7–8) – should now be mainly found, and particularly so after the referendum and the strengthening of the hard-Eurosceptic fringe of the parliamentary party.

However, sovereignist claims are not only the preserve of the Tory party. Under the leadership of Jeremy Corbyn, the Labour Party's flirting with anti-globalisation, 'Bennite' positions typical of the early 1980s appear to be in line with the protectionist policies endorsed by left-wing populist parties elsewhere in Europe.

Labour's studied ambiguity on Brexit (cf. Diamond, 2018) – with the leadership neither endorsing a 'Leave' position (in line with Corbyn's past position as backbencher), nor supporting 'Remain' or a soft version of Brexit in opposition to the government – probably paid off in the 2017 General Election, allowing Labour to keep seats in key 'Leave' marginals. Opposition to the EU in some parts of the Labour party has come in the form of a traditional socialist position, with the EU representing a system of deregulated capitalism and austerity. Based on these considerations, and in contrast to the Conservative party, we would expect the Labour party to mainly articulate an economic-sovereigntist position in its discourse.

4. Research design

In order to investigate the presence of (different types of) sovereignism in the main British parties, we analyse in depth their political discourse. We focus on parliamentary speeches on EU matters delivered by Conservative and Labour representatives in the House of Commons in the 2015–16, 2016–17, and 2017–18 parliamentary sessions, covering the entire period from the 2015 General Election to the end of October 2017 (for details, see Table A in the online Appendix).

Debates were retrieved from Hansard, the online database of verbatim reports of debates in the House of Commons, based on selected keywords, such as 'Brexit', or 'European Union'. Debates were selected from their official title and then manually scanned: only those whose content explicitly referred to key issues and events related to the process of European integration were included in our sample. Then we used a Python script to automate the procedure of retrieval and extraction of parliamentary speeches from the Parliamentary Hansard and build a machine-readable collection of speeches (or *corpus*) already divided by political party and by Member of Parliament (MP). In total, we collected and coded a corpus of 4,008 speeches (1,586 delivered by Labour and 2,422 by Conservative MPs).

Table 2. Keywords associated with sovereignism.

Sovereignism	Keywords
Economic	market, trade, tariff, membership, austerity, fiscal, monetary, EMU, Eurozone, Euro
National	Brexit, European Union, control, sovereignty, borders, national interest, immigration, Euroscepticism, supranational, Schengen
Populist	people, elite, bureaucracy, technocrats, establishment, accountability, legitimacy, European Council, European Commission, Juncker
Civic	citizens, democracy, national parliament, representation, electoral system, government, public services, institutions, civic, reforms
Cultural	values, traditions, identity, diversity, culture, multicultural, multi-ethnic, British, law and order, security

The empirical investigation was based on the Corpus-Assisted Discourse Studies (CADS) methodology that allows a fine-grained analysis of large text corpora by merging quantitative and qualitative methods in an iterative process (Partington, 2010). First, following a deductive approach to the discovery of themes (Ryan & Bernard, 2003, p. 88), we identified some keywords pertaining to the semantic domain of each of the above-mentioned sub-dimensions of sovereignism (Table 2 below).[1] Then, we looked at the absolute frequency of each keyword in both Labour and Conservative speeches, to roughly compare the relevance of each dimension between them (for a similar approach, see Ryan & Weisner, 1996). Finally, we expanded the analysis to the larger stretches of text containing these keywords, to capture the position (positive or negative) and the arguments associated with them by MPs. Only those sentences containing a sovereignist/anti-sovereignist message were coded, according to some inductively defined categories (cf. Table B in the online Appendix). The tool used for this analysis is MaxQDA, a software programme for mixed-method text analysis.

5. Empirical analysis

5.1. Intra and inter-party comparison

This section aims to assess both the relevance and the attributes of sovereigntist claims in the political discourse of the two major British parties. Figure 1 below provides a first quantitative glimpse. As expected, it shows that national and populist dimensions of sovereignism prevail in Conservative MPs' speeches, while – more surprisingly – it is the civic type of sovereignism that prevails in the Labour Party. Indeed, most sovereigntist claims made by Conservative representatives fall into two categories: 'the will of the people must be respected' (137 occurrences) and 'taking back control' (149). By contrast, the vast bulk of sovereigntist claims voiced by Labour delegates fall into the 'parliamentary sovereignty' category (149). Interestingly, cultural sovereignism, intended as an envisaged threat posed by alien cultures to a supposedly homogeneous and cohesive society, is not salient in our sample. This is probably due to the nature of the analysed debates: MPs mainly refer to Schengen and the freedom of movement of EU citizens, rather than to immigration from extra-EU countries. Moreover, the governing party is internally divided over the costs and benefits of immigration. Some Conservative MPs advocate the end of 'uncontrolled immigration' (14) in order to put the interest of 'British citizens first' (17), while other Tory MPs acknowledge the benefits that EU immigrants bring to the British economy (19).

Figure 2 below shows how the use of different types of sovereigntist claims by Conservative and Labour MPs varies over time. In the case of Conservative representatives, the

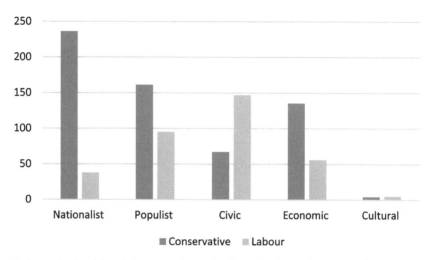

Figure 1. Sovereignist claims in Conservative and Labour MPs' speeches. Note: the y-axis reports the absolute number of claims

number of segments of text coded either as national or populist sovereignism increases considerably after the referendum, with national sovereignism remarkably outnumbering the other categories. In particular, the number of segments coded as 'national sovereignism' more than tripled (from 52 up to 184), while those coded as 'populist sovereignism' rose from 37 up to 124. In the case of Labour, the number of segments coded as 'economic sovereignism' prevails before the Brexit referendum (69 coded segments), while after the referendum, 'civic sovereignism' is the most populated category. The number of segments coded as populist sovereignism also increases after the referendum, albeit moderately. Conversely, the number of segments coded as national sovereignism decreases.

When looking at the keywords associated with each of the above-mentioned categories of sovereignism (Table 3 below), it is worth noting that the main issues identified by Conservative MPs are the 'people' (mentioned 1589 times), the 'European Union' (1078), 'British' (649), 'trade' (534), 'market' (350), and 'membership' (315). When exploring these statements in depth, a link emerges between national and populist sovereignism and support for Brexit. Indeed, Brexiteers endorse much of the Eurosceptic populist rhetoric to refer both to the EU power-grab vis-à-vis the UK and to the lack of democracy at the EU level. In addition, they invoke the 'will of the people', conceived as a homogeneous monolith, conveniently ignoring the 62.5 per cent of the electorate made up of 'remainers' and those who abstained from voting in the referendum (Freeden, 2017, p. 4). Such a type of sovereignism is well represented by the quote below:

> Many of us feel that the EU as currently constituted is thoroughly undemocratic. It stifles and prevents the will of a once-sovereign people from being properly expressed. It means that a Government cannot be elected on a prospectus that they can implement in all respects, because the European Union will not let them do so. Above all, the European Union represents the past: it is holding us back. It is something from the last century. [...] Let us get rid of these myths [...] being out of the EU or in a better and new relationship with the EU is the future: it means [...] above all, restore the sovereignty of the British people ...

John Redwood MP, EU Referendum Bill, 09/06/2015

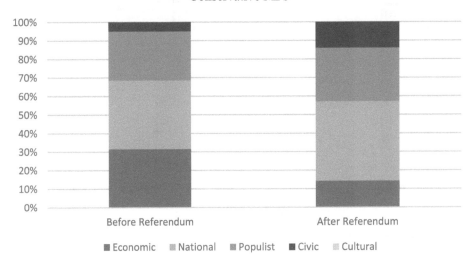

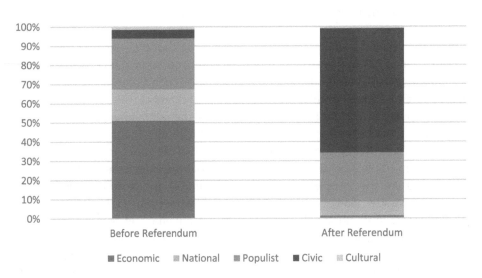

Figure 2. Types of sovereignist claims (2015–17).

When digging into economic sovereignism, it emerges how the Conservative parliamentary party is divided over the optimal post-Brexit relationship with the EU. On the one side, and in line with a historical 'hyperglobalist' Eurosceptical strand within British Conservatism, Brexiteers believe that the UK will be better off by leaving the single market (64 occurrences), as it will regain its place in the world as a global, trading nation, traditionally connected with the English-speaking world and the Commonwealth (33 occurrences). For instance:

> I sincerely believe that this process [Brexit] is not a triumph of nationalism, or of us being apart from them. It is quite the opposite: part of a new internationalism and recognition of our common

Table 3. Sub-dimensions of sovereignism by political party with most frequent keywords.

		Conservative Party	Labour Party
1	National	European Union (1078)	Brexit (567)
		Brexit (290)	European Union (562)
		Control (179)	Immigration (156)
2	Populist	People (1589)	People (183)
		Establishment (21)	Accountability (39)
		Elite (2)	European Commission (25)
3	Civic	Citizens (311)	Government (1664)
		Democracy (123)	Citizens (225)
		Accountability (13)	Democracy (106)
4	Economic	Trade (535)	Market (302)
		Market (350)	Trade (294)
		Membership (315)	Membership (224)
5	Cultural	British (649)	British (356)
		Security (105)	Security (109)
		Culture (26)	Migrants (32)

Note: top three keywords by analytical category ranked by relative importance. Absolute frequency in parenthesis. Total words: 488.775 (CON), 342.938 (LAB).

> citizenship of the whole world. We stand ready to break free of the protectionist barriers erected by the EU that have so damaged much of the third world, and rejoin the world at large.
>
> Sir Edward Leigh MP, EU (Notification of Withdrawal) Bill, 31/01/2017

Conversely, Conservative 'Remain' MPs stress the economic benefits of EU membership (59 occurrences) and claim that any trade agreement negotiated as an external partner of the EU will be less favourable to the UK than the current membership of the single market (56 occurrences). This is shown by the excerpt below:

> I think that the British benefited more from the single market than any other member state. It has contributed to our comparative economic success today.
>
> Kenneth Clarke MP, EU (Notification of Withdrawal) Bill, 31/01/2017

Among Labour MPs, by contrast, the keywords associated with sovereignist claims are the 'government' (1664 occurrences), 'Brexit' (567), the 'European Union' (562), 'British' (356), 'market' (302), and 'trade' (294). The Labour Party's main target of opposition is the Government, and civic-sovereignist arguments are used to defend the principles of British parliamentary democracy. The official position of the Labour party is to leave the EU, but several MPs stress the need to do so respecting the role of Parliament and opposing any power grab by the Government, such as, for example, in the debate on the so-called 'Henry VIII' clauses in the European Union (Withdrawal) Bill, which enable ministers to convert EU laws into UK law by using secondary legislation, over which parliament has little say.[2] In the words of one Labour MP:

> The Bill does the opposite of what people expected for parliamentary democracy and the enhancement of our courts [...]. The Prime Minister talks about British values and there are no more fundamental British values than parliamentary democracy and the rule of law.
>
> Geraint Davies MP, EU (Withdrawal) Bill, 11/09/2017

It is worth noting that Labour members subvert the national-sovereignist arguments typically used by Brexiteers, particularly the 'take back control' claim, and use them to demand clarity and accountability through the Brexit negotiations to the government.

Those who wanted to leave talked about giving the British people control – taking back control. Why, then, are we producing a Bill that will, effectively, give that control to the Government of the day, to make decisions behind closed doors, and not to this Parliament, which represents the democratic will of the people?

David Lammy MP, EU (Withdrawal) Bill, 11/09/2017

Similarly, Labour MPs use terms pertaining to the populist lexicon, but to stress the principles of parliamentary democracy. They talk in the name of those British people that did not vote in favour of Brexit and that equally deserve to have a say on the post-Brexit arrangements. Some MPs, such as the Shadow Brexit Secretary, Keir Starmer, openly advocate for a second referendum and for extending Article 50 to delay Brexit. As another Labour MP argues:

I therefore put it to the House that people now feel that they have not had their reasonable expectations fulfilled, which is why, although I accept the vote to leave in principle, I believe there should be a vote – a final say – of the people on the exit package for Britain. Such a vote would allow the people to decide whether that package meets their reasonable expectations and whether it is better than currently being in the EU – if they do not agree, they can stay.

Geraint Davies MP, EU (Notification of Withdrawal) Bill, 31/01/2017

Yet, when looking at the themes that Labour MPs associate with economic sovereignism, contrary to what we expected, there is little evidence of traditional socialist positions. The overwhelming majority of Labour MPs stress the economic disadvantages of leaving the EU, as in the examples below:

Even on the optimistic assumption that we can sign trade agreements all over the world, this does not even come close to making up for the loss of the single market.

David Lammy MP, EU (Notification of Withdrawal) Bill, 31/01/2017

Our continued membership of the single market, along with our ability to stay in the European customs union, is the most important issue for our country. It is about jobs and trade, but it is also about tackling austerity and investing in our schools and hospitals.

Heidi Alexander MP, EU (Withdrawal) Bill, 11/09/2017

Moreover, most Labour MPs claim that the UK's membership to the EU has increased workers' rights (for example trough the Workers' Agency Directive and the Parental Leave Directive) and they fear that Brexit is a project led by Conservative Brexiteers to foster neoliberal policies, such as cuts in taxes and public spending. In other words, the majority of Labours' anti-austerity discourses are addressed against the Conservative government:

The previous Labour Government signed up to the social chapter, ensuring that every worker won the right to four weeks' paid holiday […]. Voting to leave the EU could put at risk hard-won rights, because we know that some of the biggest cheerleaders for Brexit see protections for ordinary British workers as red tape to be binned.

Caroline Flint MP, EU Membership: Economic Benefits, 15/06/2016

They [the Government] threaten to create a low-tax, low-public-service haven on the coast of Europe if we do not get a trade deal with the EU, but that is precisely the kind of UK that they want, free from what they see as the constraints of employment rights and environmental protection.

> Christian Matheson MP, EU (Notification of Withdrawal) Bill, 01/02/2017

Of course, the most Eurosceptic Labour MPs, such as Kate Hoey and Kelvin Hopkins, argue for the economic benefits of leaving the EU, in order to 'take back control' of a relevant share of British resources and transfer the decision-making power over national economic policies to a democratically elected Government, rather than to the Brussels-led technocratic institutions.

> The CAP is nonsense. We ought to abolish it and repatriate agricultural policy to member states. We can decide in our own country which parts of agriculture should be subsidised and to what extent, and we can decide where and when we buy food.

> Kelvin Hopkins MP, European Union (Finance) Bill, 23/06/2015

5.2. Classifying MPs

Looking further inside the parties, we have classified Conservative and Labour MPs according to their framing strategies. By counting how many times a given MP is associated with one of the codes expressing sovereignism claims, we have identified four groups of parliamentarians. A first cluster is composed of 'national-sovereignist' MPs, who advocate national sovereignty. They oppose the EU's power grab vis-à-vis Britain's sovereignty and support Brexit as a means to 'take back control' over national borders, the welfare system, and several policy areas, such as agriculture and manufacturing. Among Conservatives, David Davis (with 44 per cent of the coded segments associated with him expressing national sovereignism), Ian Duncan Smith (40 per cent), and John Redwood (36.3 per cent) are the most prominent members. Kelvin Hopkins (67 per cent) is the most representative Labour member of this group.

A second group is composed of 'economic-sovereignist' parliamentarians, namely those MPs that stress the economic advantages of leaving the EU or, alternatively, the economic costs of EU membership, without necessarily advocating for a repatriation of EU competencies. The most representative among them are David Gauke (60 per cent) and Sir Edward Leigh (46.1 per cent) in the Conservative Party, and Barbara Keeley (70 per cent) among Labour MPs. However, while the latter is particularly vocal before the referendum and argues for a significant review of the EU budget priorities, the former mainly articulate economic sovereignism in terms of the economic benefits of being outside the common market and being able to negotiate free-trade agreements with third countries once exiting the EU.

Civic sovereignism is mainly articulated in terms of respect for the Westminster model of democracy. Among Labour MPs, Yvette Cooper (80 per cent), the Brexit shadow minister, Keir Starmer (62 per cent), Chris Leslie (50 per cent), David Lammy (37.5 per cent) and Hilary Benn (36.4 per cent) most often use civic- sovereigntist claims, while in the Conservative Party, Kenneth Clarke (44 per cent) and Anna Soubry (23.4 per cent) can be classified as civic sovereignists. It is worth noticing that their claims can be classified as 'sovereignist' when the emphasis is on the more appropriate procedure by which to leave the EU – for example, by emphasising the role of Parliament, or by allowing MPs to debate and amend government bills, etc. In this sense, several members of this group endorse 'soft' forms of Brexit.[3]

Finally, among Conservative MPs, Michael Gove (45.5 per cent) and George Freeman (31.5 per cent) are the ones that most frequently employ populist-sovereignist claims. On the opposing side, it is Kate Hoey (67 per cent) who best fits this category. They all criticise the democratic deficit of the EU – at times referred to as 'authoritarian bureaucracy' – and the need to respect the 'will of the people' as unequivocally expressed in the Brexit referendum.

6. Conclusions

This article has argued that sovereignism, expressed in the form of opposition to European integration, is by no means a new element in the British mainstream parties. National sovereignism has characterised (parts of) both parties since the UK considered its membership in the then European Economic Community. Economic and civic sovereignism were also part of their discourses and Eurosceptic positions. What is newer – and triggered both by the emergence of significant challenger parties (i.e. UKIP) and the use of an instrument of direct democracy such as the referendum – is the emergence of a form of populist sovereignism opposing the 'will of the [British] people' to the unresponsive Brussels bureaucracy. To be sure, elements of populist sovereignism have been present in the political debate since at least the early 1990s, with the Maastricht debate and the emergence of a Referendum Party. However, the context of Brexit has made the populist facet of sovereignism much more visible and significant.

The analysis of the parliamentary speeches on EU issues delivered by representatives of the Conservative and Labour parties in the House of Commons from 2015 to October 2017 has shown that different types of sovereignist claims co-exist in the British parliamentary parties. Populism has become an important theme of sovereignist claims in the Conservative Party. In particular, Brexiteers articulate a strong opposition to the European Union polity and present themselves as representatives of the 'true' popular voice, politically constructed as a homogeneous unity – the 'will of the people' – in favour of Brexit. The combination of national and populist claims characterises the Tories' sovereigntist discourses.

By contrast, civic sovereignism is predominant in the discourse of Labour MPs after the referendum. More specifically, Labour MPs play the role of watchdogs of parliamentary democracy, opposing all those measures put in place by the government to reduce the scrutiny power of parliament and strengthen the executive. If the end of EU membership is in principle accepted, it should not be an opportunity for a power grab by the government. Of course, some Labour MPs also go beyond civic sovereignism, questioning the very choice of Brexit (e.g. demanding a second referendum). Yet, this aspect goes beyond the focus (and the data) of this article.

Finally, it is worth emphasising that, contrary to what was initially hypothesised, there is little evidence of protectionist, anti-market positions among Labour MPs. Some tentative explanations can be suggested. First, the analysis focuses on the parliamentary Labour party, which is the least likely supporter of more radical economic policies – indeed, a mild supporter of the party leader *tout court*. Had the analysis focused on the 'party on the ground' – addressing speeches delivered in Northern constituencies, for example – results may have been different. Second, the party strategy may have changed in the period here analysed. If electoral considerations led to an emphasis on economic sovereignism – from a leftist perspective – in the run-up to the referendum, in the period after the referendum the Labour Party concentrated on an 'orderly' delivery of Brexit, criticising the government for its (mis)-management of the process.

Needless to say, this article deals with the ongoing process of Brexit, and party positions – and here specifically the claims made by MPs – are not only formed endogenously, but also in relation to the progress (or lack thereof) of the negotiations with the EU. As these negotiations will outlast any official Brexit day, the strength of different types of sovereignist claims (and possibly anti-sovereignist claims) will continue to vary both within and across the parties.

Notes

1. For the sake of comparability, we have limited our semantic 'dictionaries' to ten key words for each sub-dimension of sovereignism.
2. Civic sovereignist claims often overlap with support for soft forms of Brexit.
3. In some cases, civic arguments are explicit endorsements of EU institutions and policies. Such 'remain' positions are, of course, not classified as 'sovereignist'.

References

Aslanidis, P. (2018). Measuring populist discourse with semantic text analysis: An application on grassroots populist mobilization. *Quality and Quantity, 52*, 1241–1263.

Baker, D., Gamble, A., & Seawright, D. (2002). Sovereign nations and global markets: Modern British Conservatism and hyperglobalism. *British Journal of Politics and International Relations, 4*(3), 399–428.

Baldini, G., Bressanelli, E., & Massetti, E. (2018). Who is in control? Brexit and the Westminster model. *Political Quarterly, 89*(4), 537–544. OnlineFirst.

Bale, T. (2018). Who leads and who follows? The symbiotic relationship between UKIP and the Conservatives – and populism and Euroscepticism. *Politics, 38*(3), 263–277.

Basile, L., & Mazzoleni, O. (2020). Sovereignist wine in populist bottles? An introduction. *European Politics and Society, 21*(2), 151–162.

Bogdanor, V. (2016). Europe and the sovereignty of the people. *Political Quarterly, 87*(3), 348–351.

Brubaker, R. (2017). Why populism? *Theory and Society, 46*, 357–385.

Cowley, P., & Norton, P. (1999). Rebels and rebellions: Conservative MPs in the 1992 Parliament. *British Journal of Politics and International Relations, 1*(1), 84–105.

Cowley, P., & Stuart, M. (2010). Where has all the trouble gone? British intra-party parliamentary divisions during the Lisbon ratification. *British Politics, 5*(2), 133–148.

Crines, A., & Heppell, T. (2017). Rhetorical style and issue emphasis within the conference speeches of UKIP's Nigel Farage 2010-2014. *British Politics, 12*(2), 231–249.

Crines, A., Jeffery, D., & Heppell, T. (2018). The British Labour Party and leadership election mandate(s) of Jeremy Corbyn: Patterns of opinion and opposition within the parliamentary Labour Party. *Journal of Elections, Public Opinion and Parties, 28*(3), 361–379.

Curtice, J. (2017). Why leave won the UK's EU referendum. *Journal of Common Market Studies, 55*, 19–37.

Diamond, P. (2018). Euro-caution vs. Euro-fanaticism? The Labour Party's 'constructive ambiguity' on Brexit and the European Union. In P. Diamond, P. Nedergaard, & B. Rosamond (Eds.), *Routledge Handbook of the politics of Brexit* (pp. 167–178). London: Routledge.

Freeden, M. (2017). After the Brexit referendum: Revisiting populism as an ideology. *Journal of Political Ideologies, 22*(1), 1–11.

Gamble, A. (2003). *Between Europe and America. The future of British politics*. Basingstoke: Palgrave.

George, S. (1998). *An awkward partner. Britain in the European community*. Oxford: Oxford University Press.

Gifford, C. (2014). *The making of Eurosceptic Britain* (2nd ed). Farnham: Ashgate.

Grande, E., & Schwarzbözl, T. (2017). *Politicizing Europe in the UK*. Dynamics of inter-party competition and intra-party conflict. Paper prepared for the Conference 'Rejected Europe. Beloved Europe. Cleavage Europe' at the European University Institute, Florence, May 18–19.

Grant, C. (2008). *Why is Britain Eurosceptic?* London: Centre for European Reform.

Heinisch, R., & Mazzoleni, O. (2017). Analysing and explaining populism: Bringing frame, actor and context back in. In R. Heinisch, C. Holtz-Bacha, & O. Mazzoleni (Eds.), *Political populism* (pp. 105–122). Baden-Baden: Nomos.

Heppell, T., Crines, A., & Jeffery, D. (2017). The United Kingdom referendum on European Union membership: The voting of conservative parliamentarians. *Journal of Common Market Studies, 55*(4), 762–778.

Hobolt, S. (2016). The Brexit vote: A divided nation, a divided continent. *Journal of European Public Policy, 23*(9), 1259–1277.

Hooghe, L., & Marks, G. (2012). Politicization. In E. Jones, A. Menon, & S. Weatherhill (Eds.), *Oxford Handbook of the European Union* (pp. 840–853). Oxford: Oxford University Press.

Jackson, D., Thorsen, E., & Wring, E. (eds.). (2016). *EU referendum analysis 2016: Media, voters and the campaign*. Poole: Political Studies Association.

Judge, D. (2005). *Political institutions in the United Kingdom*. Oxford: Oxford University Press.

Kallis, A. (2018). Populism, sovereignism, and the unlikely ReEmergence of the territorial nation-state. *Fudan Journal of Humanity and Social Science, 11*, 285–302.

Kriesi, H., Grande, E., Dolezal, M., Helbling, M., Höglinger, D., Hutter, S., & Wüest, B. (2012). *Political conflict in Western Europe*. Cambridge; New York: Cambridge University Press.

Kriesi, H., Grande, E., Lachat, R., Dolezal, M., Bornschier, S., & Frey, T. (eds.). (2008). *West European politics in the Age of globalization*. Cambridge: Cambridge University Press.

Leuffen, D., Rittberger, B., & Schimmelfennig, F. (2012). *Differentiated integration. Explaining variation in the European Union*. Basingstoke: Palgrave.

Lynch, P., & Whitaker, R. (2018). Where there is discord, can they bring harmony? Managing intra-party dissent on European integration in the conservative party. *The British Journal of Politics and International Relations, 15*, 317–339.

Menon, A., & Salter, J. P. (2016). Brexit: Initial reflections. *International Affairs, 6*, 1297–1318.

Mudde, C. (2007). *Populist radical right parties in Europe*. Cambridge: Cambridge University Press.

Norton, P. (1980). *Dissension in the house of commons. 1974-1979*. Oxford: Clarendon Press.

Pareschi, A., & Albertini, A. (2018). Immigration, elites and the European Union. The framing of populism in the discourse of Farage's UKIP. *Comunicazione Politica, 2*, 247–272.

Partington, A. (2010). Modern diachronic corpus-assisted discourse studies (MD-CADS) on UK newspapers: An overview of the project. *Corpora, 5*(2), 83–108.

Ryan, G. W., & Bernard, R. H. (2003). Techniques to identify themes. *Field Methods, 15*(1), 85–109.

Ryan, G. W., & Weisner, T. (1996). Analyzing words in brief descriptions: Fathers and mothers describe their children. *Cultural Anthropology Methods Journal, 8*(3), 13–16.

Sandbrook, D. (2018). 'Enoch Powell speaks for Britain': The press, the public and the speech. *The Political Quarterly, 89*(3), 392–399.

Saunders, R. (2018). *Yes to Europe, The 1975 referendum and seventies Britain*. Cambridge: Cambridge University Press.

Schmidt, V. (2006). Adapting to Europe: Is it harder for Britain? *British Journal of Politics and International Relations, 8*, 15–33.

Wellings, B., & Vines, E. (2016). Populism and sovereignty: The EU Act and the in-out referendum, 2010–2015. *Parliamentary Affairs, 69*(2), 309–326.

'For whom the sovereignist bell tolls?' Individual determinants of support for sovereignism in ten European countries

Linda Basile [iD], Rossella Borri and Luca Verzichelli

ABSTRACT

Sovereignism and populism are increasingly making headlines, but their nature and definition still remain controversial. Moreover, while literature has often treated the two concepts separately, they are increasingly associated in the current representations and narratives of political events. In this paper, we argue that sovereignism is one of the recurrent and core themes of populism, and pre-exists it. We conceive of sovereignism as a multidimensional concept, based upon a three-fold space, identifying its political, cultural, and economic expressions. By using survey data, we first empirically assess the existence of these three latent dimensions; then, we test a number of hypotheses to explain public opinion's support for each kind of sovereignist claim.

Results show that some predictors, like conspiracy thinking, party-cueing, and political efficacy, are common to all three dimensions. Nonetheless, the use of media, left-right ideological orientations, and socio-demographic background do not have the same impact, thus confirming the theoretical distinction of these dimensions. Moreover, we find that populist parties can skilfully capitalize on people's grievances, by fostering sovereignist attitudes among their voters. However, the intrinsic heterogeneity of sovereignist supporters would make it difficult for one single movement to exploit the three dimensions and mobilize voters on all of them.

Introduction

The tendency of some political actors to depict themselves as champions of the sovereign people, against a privileged and corrupt elite, is commonly recognized as one of the main defining features of populism (Kriesi, 2014; Mudde, 2016 and 2004; Abts & Rummens, 2007; Canovan, 1999). This rhetoric can be articulated in different ways, featuring the multifaceted nature of the populist phenomenon. But what *all* these different discursive constructions have in common is an evocative claim of full control over decision-making by a group, or community – the 'people', the 'we', though loosely defined – as opposed to an equally vaguely defined elite: in other words, the recovery of people's *sovereignty*.

Sovereignty therefore represents a core, recurrent theme of populism (Basile & Mazzoleni, 2020), 'the critical common political denominator for all populist platforms and parties across Europe' (Kallis, 2018, p. 286). It is precisely this appeal to the people's sovereignty, in its different configurations, which confers the conceptual specification, or 'the content', to the 'thin' populist ideology.

Moreover, sovereignist claims can assume several forms, according to which idea of 'people' they refer to, and they might not necessarily coexist altogether in the same political discourse, thus featuring a variable-geometry pattern. This pervasive presence of sovereignist arguments in the populist discourse has contributed to blurring the distinction between the two concepts, while emphasizing their inextricable relationship (Kallis, 2018; Kelly, 2017). Against this backdrop, this article has a twofold aim. Firstly, it unfolds the concept of sovereignism, which we conceive as multidimensional, and – using public opinion survey data – it advances methods for its conceptualization and measurement. Secondly, it explores the determinants of public opinion's support for sovereignist claims.

Our argument is that variation on individual preferences for sovereignist arguments is affected by conspiratorial, paranoid beliefs, the sense of political inefficacy, and the ideological affinity with those political actors that usually feed on sovereignist themes – namely, populist parties. In particular, we expect that populist parties are exercising a cueing effect (Bullock, 2011; Dalton, Beck, & Huckfeldt, 1998) on their followers, by fuelling people's grievances and suspicion against the elites, with the related willingness to 'take back the control' of decision making, as well as by stimulating and reinforcing latent feelings of political inefficacy among citizens.

The paper is organized as follows. The first section provides a theoretical framework for the operationalization of sovereignism as a multidimensional concept and its relationship with populism. The second section presents a number of hypotheses, grounded in theory, to explain individuals' support for sovereignist claims. The third section presents the variables, and their operationalization, that are used for the empirical analysis conducted in the fourth section. The last section outlines the main concluding remarks emerging from the research.

Populism meets sovereignism

The contemporary conceptualization of sovereignty features three core elements: first, it refers to a *mutually exclusive territory*, which mostly coincides with the national state, where sovereignty is exerted; second, it is the expression of the *popular will*; third, it relies upon the *mechanisms of representative democracy* (Sassen, 1996; Basile & Mazzoleni, 2020).

The processes of globalization and European integration have upended these cornerstones of modern sovereignty, as national states have lost their exclusive authority over their territory. Meanwhile, contemporary challenges, like the financial or migration crises, have exposed national governments' capacity to address people's uncertainties and concerns with effective policies. With the centres of power so dispersed and deterritorialized, it is indeed increasingly difficult to find, at the national level, adequate answers to global problems; at the same time, the hard-to-accept sacrifices imposed by too distant supranational policy-making structures are perceived as inadequate to respond to internal and external challenges. This has undermined the credibility of both national and supranational elites to adequately represent the popular will. This context of uncertainty and insecurity has created a fertile terrain for the rise of political actors promoting alternative solutions to the present configuration of Western liberal democracy, namely populist movements and parties.

Populism is commonly described as a fuzzy, multifaceted political phenomenon (Mudde & Kaltwasser, 2012), lacking any common ideological denominator that could be used to understand its nature. It can assume different forms, is usually very context-specific, and moves comfortably across both sides of the left-right continuum. It is indeed described as an 'empty shell which can be filled and made meaningful by whatever is poured into it' (Mény & Surel, 2002, p. 6). This is the reason why one of its most commonly accepted definitions is that of a 'thin-centred ideology' (Mudde, 2004, p. 543). The peculiar nature of populism, however, can be found precisely in the vagueness of the notion of 'the people' or, most notably, in the representation of the populist 'heartland'; an idealized, virtuous world 'as it was' and is no more, 'something that is felt rather than reasoned' (Taggart, 2004, p. 274). This interpretation of reality, referring to an archetypal sovereign territory, delineates the values and the themes of each populist discourse (Taggart, 2004), which advocates *the sovereign rule of the people* as a homogeneous body (Abts & Rummens, 2007, p. 407).

The appeal to the sovereign people is therefore paramount for *all* kinds of populism (Kriesi, 2014, p. 362), as they re-elaborate sovereignty claims around the ideological construction of the antagonism between 'the people' and 'the corrupted elites'. However, the actual sovereign people they appeal to varies sharply from one specific articulation of the heartland to the other. Scholars have indeed argued that, 'as a "thin" ideology, populism can easily be combined with different "thick" ideologies' (Mudde, 2004, p. 544), 'which elaborate the common core of the sovereign people in various ways – in terms of class, nation, 'losers' of different stripes' (Kriesi, 2014, p. 369).

Drawing on this literature, we expect to isolate three distinct, though not necessarily mutually exclusive dimensions of sovereignty claims: *political sovereignism,* focusing on a critique of the mechanisms of democratic representation, and promoting more direct, participatory practices (Kriesi, 2014); *cultural sovereignism,* based on the defence of national identity against the threats posed by multiculturalism, globalization, and immigration; and *economic sovereignism,* blaming international and supranational institutions for economic difficulties, and claiming for states, the regaining of control over economic policies and markets.

Populism then re-elaborates on these three dimensions of sovereignism, by providing *ideological constructions of the people against the elite.* Indeed, as suggested by Kriesi (2014, p. 362), the three dimensions of sovereignty correspond to the three conceptions of 'the people' as idealized by populism. In particular, the 'economic people', or the people as a class, identifies the community of disadvantaged people – those who have been harmed by economic globalization – as a homogeneous entity opposed to the economic, globalized elite of the international markets. The 'cultural people' is the national community, sharing common experiences and culture, although they might be just the product of socially constructed beliefs, rather than actual common features; this ethnically homogeneous group – or group perceived as such – is against the multiculturalist elites, promoting a pluralism of ideas and cultures that would hinder the purity of the nation. Finally, the 'political people' is the purely sovereign people, the fullest authority acknowledged to the ordinary citizens, here conceived as a monolithic entity, whose will should be fully respected and enacted, against the distant, represented elites – and especially the technocratic elites in Brussels.

Figure 1 proposes a graphical representation of how populism takes over sovereignty claims.

What drives sovereignist attitudes? Theory and hypotheses

Having assessed the multidimensional nature of sovereignism and its nature as a key component of the populist discourse, we turn our attention to its potential micro-level determinants, namely the factors that explain variations in people's attitudes towards sovereignist arguments, and how they relate to the populist political ability to mobilize voters on these claims.

Our theoretical framework starts with what can be defined as 'conspiracy thinking'. As scholars argue, the populist reframing of sovereignist messages is centred on a dualist 'us' versus 'them' worldview, a hyper-simplistic binary narrative of friends and foes, good and evil, pitting the pure, sovereign people against the corrupt elites, and excluding the existence of any other possible division (Canovan, 1999; Mudde, 2004; Taggart, 2004). Psychological research supports the idea that compliance to such a Manichean rhetoric is particularly recurrent among individuals who share specific latent attitudes (Goertzel, 1994; Silva, Vegetti, & Littvay, 2017; Wood, Douglas, & Sutton, 2012) or, more precisely, a 'monological belief system' (Goertzel, 1994), making them more prone to hold mutually-supportive, conspiratorial, paranoid beliefs. Empirical studies demonstrate (Goertzel, 1994; McClosky & Chong, 1985; Oliver & Wood, 2014; Wood et al., 2012) that those people sharing these beliefs think that any given event is the result of secret conspiracies orchestrated for sinister reasons by the holders of (economic or political) powers, aiming to manipulate the unaware people. These beliefs go beyond a general lack of trust in political institutions, since they encapsulate paranoid argumentations, positing that decisions are always taken behind the scenes. That is why 'monological conspiracy thinkers' (Goertzel, 1994, p. 741) would, indeed, 'naturally begin to see authorities as fundamentally deceptive' (Wood et al., 2012, p. 2), thus casting doubts on the

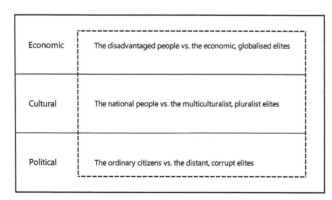

Figure 1. The three dimensions of sovereignism (outer square) and the populist reframing of sovereignist claims.

functioning of democratic institutions, as well as on the good intentions of any outsider from the homogeneous group of the 'sovereign people'.

Research has also shown that this kind of mindset is even more intense in the case of social-media users (Bessi et al., 2015; Del Vicario, Gaito, Quattrociocchi, Zignani, & Zollo, 2017).[1] It is also self-reinforcing (Bessi et al., 2015; Del Vicario et al., 2017; Flynn, Nyhan, & Reifler, 2017), to the extent that people do actually tend to seek out (and believe) information that conforms to their preferences (Bessi et al., 2015; Flynn et al., 2017). This also implies the selection of information from sources that are compatible with one's own views and which, in the case of conspiracy thinkers, are likely to further polarize the 'us' versus 'them' view (Del Vicario et al., 2017; Miller, Saunders, & Farhart, 2016).

We therefore expect to find greater support for sovereignist claims among conspiracy thinkers; we also control for the frequency of the use of different media sources from which people get their information, with social media users potentially more inclined to share self-reinforcing (conspiratorial) information:

> H1 (Conspiracy hypothesis): People endorsing conspiracy arguments and paranoid beliefs are more likely to support sovereigntist worldviews – especially among social-media users.

Our second hypothesis focuses on the impact of political efficacy on sovereignist attitudes. Political efficacy is here defined in terms of both internal and external efficacy – the former referring to an individual's sense of competence on political issues, and the latter to the belief that politicians are responsive to people's demands (Sulitzeanu-Kenan & Halperin, 2013).

Our argument points to the consequences of the economic, cultural and political changes fostered by the processes of transformation from industrial into post-industrial economies and societies, in an increasingly globalized world (Kriesi et al., 2012; Mudde, 2007). In the face of such a complex scenario, with the dispersion and deterritorialization of the centres of power, national governments and elites have reduced their responsiveness to people's concerns. These challenges have been further magnified by the complexity and opacity of decision-making processes in multi-level settings, which are often too intricate for average citizens, and by media reporting strategies about politics, which have tended in recent decades to overemphasize the most scandalous aspects of political events and politicians (Mudde, 2004, p. 553). All this has contributed to fostering the idea, firstly, that politics is too complex to play a role in, and secondly, that political decisions are usually taken behind the scenes and ordinary citizens have little, if any influence on decision making. Citizens have increasingly developed feelings of alienation from politics (Mudde, 2004), while 'this may result in a structural crisis of the feeling of being represented' (Spruyt, Keppens, & Van Droogenbroeck, 2016, p. 3). This is especially true for those social sectors, defined as 'losers of globalization' (Spruyt et al., 2016), that are less equipped to deal with such deep changes.

Recent literature has argued that low political efficacy makes people more prone to support populist actors (Kemmers, 2017; Magni, 2017; Rooduijn, van der Brug, & de Lange, 2016). Populists' appeal to bring sovereignty back to the popular will within the national territory, their marked anti-elitism and anti-institutionalism, as well as the claims for a direct and more simple politics (Mény & Surel, 2002, p. 76) might indeed respond to people's quest for having their voice heard and 'their will reflected in politics, unrestrained by regulations, laws, procedures' (Kemmers, 2017, p. 383). Although we seek to explain variation in support for sovereignist claims, rather than preferences for populist parties, these arguments can be poured into our hypothesis, if we observe that populists tend to attract voters just by promoting sovereignist solutions to global challenges, as earlier noted:

H2 (Political efficacy hypothesis): The lower the sense of (internal and external) political efficacy people have, the more they will lean towards sovereignist preferences.

Beyond people's feelings, we must observe that people do not move within a vacuum, but are rather embedded into a political system featuring a number of parties and movements, which seek to promote and mobilize voters on a vast array of policy issues and claims, including sovereignist ones. This suggests the importance of considering the cueing activity played by those political parties that are able to exacerbate existing feelings of discontent and capitalize on the quest for social change, by actively manipulating people's grievances (Minkenberg, 2000). In particular, we refer to those actors that can be grouped under the political umbrella term of populism, whose common denominator – within what is, as previously argued, an otherwise varied ideology – is represented by the reference to sovereignist claims.

There is evidence in the literature concerning the influence of political parties on public opinion (Dalton et al., 1998; Marks, 1999). When parties take stances on policy issues, people tend to follow the lead of their preferred party, either from blind loyalty, or because they consider the party a trustworthy source and therefore use party positions as a rational information shortcut (Azrout & de Vreese, 2018; Brader, Tucker, & Duell, 2013), although this cue-taking effect might vary due to individual and contextual factors (Brader et al., 2013):

H3 (Party cue-taking hypothesis): Support for sovereignist claims is higher among those people who feel close to populist parties.

Data and variables. The EUENGAGE panel survey

To address our key research questions, we use data from the EUENGAGE[2] mass-panel survey. The first wave was conducted between June and July 2016 and interviewed 21,820[3] European citizens in 10 countries (Czech Republic, France, Germany, Greece, Italy, the Netherlands, Poland, Portugal, Spain, and the United Kingdom). The second wave was conducted between June and October 2017, on a sample of 11,140[4] citizens from the first wave's pool of respondents. In this article we analyse only panel respondents, in order to use survey items from both waves.

The latent dimensions of populist sovereignism: a principal factor analysis

We conceived support for sovereignist claims – which represents our dependent variable – as an intrinsically multidimensional concept. This requires identifying the main latent dimensions underlying sovereignist claims. We thus performed a data reduction exercise, using a principal factor analysis (PFA) with promax rotation[5] to provide robust evidence to the thesis of the multidimensionality of sovereignism, by using a set of survey items that would likely capture these latent dimensions.[6] They seek to seize the three-fold space of sovereignism – political, cultural, and economic – as identified by literature, where each dimension corresponds to the particular 'sovereign people' addressed by these claims.

The screen plot obtained from the PFA suggests retaining three factors, with eigenvalues higher than 1.0, all of them appearing to be relatively distinct and interpretable according to the theory and explaining overall 67.7 per cent of total variance. We then defined factors by selecting items with factor loading higher than 0.40. Results from the PFA are shown in Table 1.

Using these items, we built three indexes by averaging the non-weighted scores on the items in each factor.[7] The first factor includes the items on citizens' perception of migrants, and that on the EU authority on migration issues, with factor loadings ranging from 0.53 to 0.83. They are used to build the index of *cultural sovereignism* (Cronbach's alpha 0.84), which relates to the promotion of an exclusionary, nationalist identity, the defence of national borders to protect the in-group community, and its purity, against 'the others' coming from outside.

The second factor is composed of the items measuring people's perception of the EU as a threat to national economy and welfare, the EU's authority on economic issues, and attitudes towards globalization. In these cases, factor loadings range from 0.46 to 0.87. They are used to build the index of *economic sovereignism* (Cronbach's alpha 0.71), measuring citizens' refusal of supranational economic integration and the globalization of the markets.

Finally, the third factor includes the items on the trust in governments, preferences for direct democracy, and satisfaction with EU democratic functioning, whose factor loadings range from 0.55 to 0.83. The index resulting from these survey questions accounts for citizens' dissatisfaction with the mechanisms of democratic representation, and the willingness to promote the popular will of the sovereign people, or the *political sovereignism* (Cronbach's alpha 0.54).[8] Lower scores on these indexes indicate support for sovereignist claims, while higher scores denote opposite, liberalist, and supranationalist views.

Since the factor analysis confirms the existence of three distinct, latent dimensions of sovereignism, we will test our hypotheses on each index, considered as separate dependent variables, according to the following models:

$$Y_1 \text{(or } Y_2, \text{ or } Y_3) = a + b1^*\text{Conspiracy} + b1\_1^*\text{Use of newspaper}$$
$$+ b1\_2^*\text{Use of social media} + b1\_3^*\text{Use of television}$$
$$+ b2^*\text{Political (internal \& external) efficacy} + b3^*\text{Party cue-taking}$$
$$+ b4^*\text{ideology (left-right)} + b5^*\text{socio} - \text{demographic background}$$
$$\text{(gender, age, education)}$$

Whereas: $Y_1 =$ cultural sovereignism, $Y_2 =$ economic sovereignism, and $Y_3 =$ political sovereignism.

Independent variables[9]

Conspiracy thinking is measured by using an index built upon a set of 9 survey questions asking for respondents' level of agreement with a number of statements casting doubts over the transparency of the functioning of democratic systems and of the political and financial elites, as well as of the media (Cronbach's alpha $= 0.85$). Lower scores on the

Table 1. Factor loadings based on a principal factor analysis with promax rotation for 14 items from the EUENGAGE panel survey 2016–2017 – weighted (N = 11,113).

	Factor 1	Factor 2	Factor 3	
Eigenvalue	4.46819	1.63114	1.17699	
% of variance explained	29.4	21.7	16.6	
	Cultural sovereignism	*Economic sovereignism*	*Political sovereignism*	*Uniqueness*
Immigrants – terrorist attack	0.8280			0.3225
Immigrants – contribute more in taxes	0.6314			0.5404
Immigration – improve our culture	0.7249			0.3644
Immigrants – religious practices	0.8253			0.3166
Immigrants – crime	0.7901			0.3473
EU vs. National authority (Migration)	0.5274			0.6439
EU as a danger to: welfare system		0.8691		0.2631
EU as a danger to: economic growth		0.8441		0.2781
Globalization		0.4640		0.6564
EU vs. National authority (Economy)		0.5279		0.5865
Satisfaction with EU democracy			0.5850	0.4654
Direct vs. representative democracy			0.6401	0.5843
Trust in [Country] government			0.8194	0.3548

Note: Factor loadings < .40 are suppressed.

index indicate higher support for conspiratorial arguments. We also use three survey items asking respondents about their weekly *use of newspapers, television, and social media* as sources of information.

Following Craig and Maggiotto (1982, pp. 89–90), we use the survey item on people's perceived influence on government to measure *external political efficacy*. It is combined with the one measuring people's perception of politicians' attention to their interests (Cronbach's alpha 0.69). External inefficacy is expressed by lower scores on this index. By contrast, we use the item on respondents' perception of the complexity in politics to measure *internal political efficacy*, as a dummy variable, in which 0 indicates political internal inefficacy, and 1 otherwise.

Measuring party cues

The cue-taking hypothesis brings into the picture the role of populist parties, their influence on public opinion, and their relationship with sovereignism.

As previously argued, under the populist label there is a plethora of different parties, from both the left and right side of the political spectrum; although thin and varied, however, their ideology features an ever-present reference to sovereignist claims and appeals to sovereign people. Accordingly, we identify populist parties by considering those actors actively promoting specific sovereignist claims in their political discourse and drawing the attention of the party system to these issues. This definition comes close to that of 'issue entrepreneurs' (Hobolt & De Vries, 2015, p. 5), namely parties that tend to heighten the attention on certain issues (i.e. to put high salience on sovereignist claims) and adopt a position on them that is substantially different from that of the average of the other parties in the party system (Hobolt & De Vries, 2015, pp. 11–12).

We followed a two-step process to operationalize a party cue-taking variable. First, using the Chapel Hill Expert Survey (CHES) FLASH 2017[10] data (Polk et al., 2017), which provides expert-based estimates of party positions and salience on several policy issues, we selected those items that are likely to tap party positions on the *political, cultural*, and *economic* dimensions of sovereignism; we then measured parties' issue entrepreneurship on sovereignist claims as a party's salience on these claims, multiplied by the distance between its position and the mean position of all parties in the system on the same issue (Hobolt & De Vries, 2015):

$$\text{Party cueing}_{(x)} = \text{Salience } (x_{\text{Pol,Cult,Eco}}) * [\text{Party position } (x_{\text{Pol,Cult,Eco}})]$$
$$- \text{ Parties' average position in country } (x_{\text{Pol,Cult,Eco}})$$

where x is represented by the CHES-based score on each of the three dimensions of sovereignism. Negative scores on these indexes correspond to a strong entrepreneurship activity played by a party on sovereignist claims, while positive scores apply to those parties that mostly campaign against these arguments.

Second, we created three variables in the mass survey dataset, by assigning the scores obtained with the CHES to the party with which the respondents identify. Figure 2 shows CHES-based party scores on the three dimensions of sovereignism across the ten countries included in our analysis.

The figure shows that only a few parties occupy the bottom 'sovereignist' area in all three dimensions: Chrysí Avgí (XA) in Greece, Partij voor de Vrijheid (PVV) in the

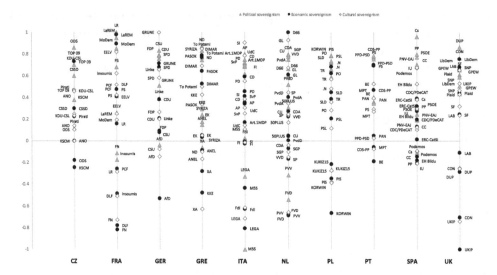

Figure 2. CHES-based party scores on the three dimensions of sovereignism.

Netherlands, the Alternative fur Deutschland (AfD) in Germany, and the Lega in Italy. In many other cases, parties present a combination of just two out of three dimensions, such as the ruling party in Poland, Prawo i Sprawiedliwość (PiS), which includes arguments related to economic and cultural sovereignism, but not the critique of the mechanisms of representative democracy (i.e. political sovereignism). By contrast, the Movimento 5 Stelle (M5S) in Italy has a strong emphasis on political sovereignism, followed by economic sovereignism, but does not pay particular attention to cultural sovereignism. This finding further supports the theoretical argument for the multidimensionality of sovereignism, which assumes a variable-geometry pattern on the supply side, thus also suggesting a similar structure on the voters' demand side.

Empirical findings

Our central argument is that sovereignism is a multidimensional concept, featuring different claims appealing to different people; nonetheless, we identified at least three features, namely conspiracy thinking, a sense of political inefficacy, and party cue-taking, that we suppose are shared by supporters of all kinds of sovereignism.

To test our hypotheses, we specified and estimated a series of nested linear-regression models for each dimension of sovereignism – political, cultural, and economic. The first model features only background variables, including gender, age, country, and education. The second and third models add people's ideological background (party cueing and left-right ideology), and people's sense of political efficacy, respectively. The last model is a composite one, including all predictor variables introduced in previous models, while adding conspiracy thinking and the frequency of the use of media.

Table 2 summarizes the performance of the four models for each dependent variable. For political and cultural sovereignism, the largest change in R^2 is observed when the variable on political efficacy is introduced, while the variables on conspiracy thinking and use of media determine a boost in the explained variance for economic sovereignism. Overall,

Table 2. Nested models to estimate sovereignist attitudes.

Models				Political sovereignism				
	F	df	df	Pr > F	R2	Change in R2	AIC	BIC
Background and context	89.76	14	11082	0	0.1018		−7825.345	−7715.628
Ideology	114.08	5	11077	0	0.1458	0.044	−8372.562	−8226.273
Efficacy	603.07	2	11075	0	0.2297	**0.0839**	−9515.712	−9354.795
Conspiracy – composite model	253.05	4	11071	0	**0.2942**	0.0645	−10478.54	−10288.37

Models				Cultural sovereignism				
	F	df	df	Pr > F	R2	Change in R2	AIC	BIC
Background and context	169.67	14	11082	0	0.1765		−2321.228	−2211.511
Ideology	423.55	5	11077	0	0.3087	0.1322	−4252.624	−4106.335
Efficacy	515.81	2	11075	0	0.3676	**0.0589**	−5236.952	−5076.035
Conspiracy – composite model	191.15	4	11071	0	**0.4084**	0.0409	**−5970.048**	**−5779.873**

Models				Economic sovereignism				
	F	df	df	Pr > F	R2	Change in R2	AIC	BIC
Background and context	84.56	14	11082	0	0.0965		−5258.198	−5148.481
Ideology	247.25	5	11077	0	0.1872	0.0907	−6422.307	−6276.019
Efficacy	320.46	2	11075	0	0.2317	0.0445	−7042.607	−6881.69
Conspiracy – composite model	449.41	4	11071	0	**0.3390**	0.1073	**−8704.302**	**−8514.127**

however, the composite models outperform the previous models in all three dependent variables, as the smaller values (i.e. the better) of the AIC and BIC values for the models that include all predictors, reveal. Accordingly, Table 3 will show only the results for the composite models, and comments will be based on them.

Conspiratorial thinking, sources of information, and sovereignist retrenchement

In line with the expectations of H1, results show that holding conspiratorial beliefs makes support for all the dimensions of sovereignism more likely. In particular, the magnitude of the coefficients for all the three dependent variables reveals that when people shift by one unit along the conspiracy index, then, *ceteris paribus*, the endorsement of sovereignist arguments increases, respectively, by: 0.29 (political and cultural sovereignism), up to 0.41 (economic sovereignism). Indeed, the underlying perception that the decision-makers mostly work behind the scenes, is consistent with – and is likely to reinforce – the idea of 'bringing the power back to the people' that is typical of political sovereignism. Likewise, the recent economic and migration upheavals would foster the perception that the current challenges are the outcome of the ruling activity played by distant, shady elites who secretly pull the strings – and this would make more appealing the sovereignist retrenchment within national borders, to protect a country's economy (economic sover-eignism), or a nation's culture and identity (cultural sovereignism).

Contrary to the expectations of a self-reinforcing effect between media consumption and conspiratorial beliefs, the coefficients for the variable on the frequency of the use of social media reveal that a high exposure to social media would decrease support for political and cultural sovereignist claims, although with limited impact, while it is not

Table 3. OLS Models.

		Political sovereignism^		Cultural sovereignism		Economic sovereignism	
		B	s.e.	B	s.e.	B	s.e.
Socio-demographic and geographical context	Gender (1 = Male; 0 = Female)	0.00416	(0.00301)	−0.00781*	(0.00369)	0.00528	(0.00326)
	Age	−0.00202	(0.00803)	−0.0239*	(0.00982)	−0.0264**	(0.00867)
	Education (Ref. Low education: primary – some high education)						
	High school	0.0138*	(0.00550)	0.0321***	(0.00674)	0.000498	(0.00596)
	Graduate	0.0189**	(0.00586)	0.0490***	(0.00718)	0.0127*	(0.00635)
	Post-graduate	0.0217***	(0.00641)	0.0672***	(0.00785)	0.0337***	(0.00694)
	Country (Ref. Czech Republic)						
	France	0.000137	(0.00625)	0.186***	(0.00760)	−0.00404	(0.00670)
	Germany	0.0530***	(0.00618)	0.212***	(0.00758)	0.0286***	(0.00669)
	Greece	−0.0758***	(0.00638)	0.192***	(0.00786)	−0.0417***	(0.00691)
	Italy	0.0181**	(0.00621)	0.260***	(0.00741)	0.0191**	(0.00659)
	The Netherlands	0.0496***	(0.00630)	0.151***	(0.00777)	−0.0127	(0.00679)
	Poland	0.0614***	(0.00635)	0.130***	(0.00785)	0.123***	(0.00692)
	Portugal	0.0223**	(0.00706)	0.267***	(0.00868)	0.0128	(0.00765)
	Spain	0.0260***	(0.00621)	0.283***	(0.00770)	0.0705***	(0.00672)
	United Kingdom	0.0254***	(0.00627)	0.236***	(0.00781)	0.0346***	(0.00713)
	Party cue						
Ideology (H3)	Political sovereignist cues	−0.0729***	(0.00504)				
	Cultural sovereignist cues			−0.105***	(0.00465)		
	Economic sovereignist cues					−0.0739***	(0.00398)
	Left right ideology (Ref: Left)						
	Center-left	0.0466***	(0.00887)	−0.0463***	(0.0109)	0.0195*	(0.00962)
	Center	0.0576***	(0.00830)	−0.138***	(0.0102)	−0.00946	(0.00900)
	Center-right	0.0649***	(0.00890)	−0.195***	(0.0112)	−0.0377***	(0.00965)
	Right	0.0430***	(0.0108)	−0.231***	(0.0135)	−0.112***	(0.0117)
Political efficacy (H2)	External efficacy	0.143***	(0.00695)	0.160***	(0.00851)	0.0546***	(0.00752)
	Internal efficacy	−0.0445***	(0.00319)	−0.0149***	(0.00390)	−0.00468	(0.00345)
Conspiracy thinking and use of media (H1)	Conspiracy thinking (0 = high conspiracy;1 = low conspiracy)	0.279***	(0.00884)	0.294***	(0.0107)	0.405***	(0.00959)
	Frequency of media use						
	Social media	0.0101*	(0.00414)	0.0211***	(0.00507)	0.00211	(0.00448)
	Newspaper	0.00665	(0.00464)	0.0160**	(0.00568)	−0.00846	(0.00502)
	Television	0.00885	(0.00480)	−0.0230***	(0.00588)	−0.00634	(0.00520)
	Constant	0.181***	(0.0114)	0.170***	(0.0140)	0.263***	(0.0124)
	N	11097		11097		11097	
	R-sq	0.294		0.408		0.339	
	Mean VIF	2.3		2.32		2.30	

***p < 0.001; **p < 0.01; *p < 0.05.
Note: ^ Dependent variables range from 0 (high support for sovereignist claims) to 1 (low support for sovereignist claims).

even statistically significant in the case of economic sovereignism. This finding, however, comes as no surprise, since the use of new media cross-cuts people's preferences: the most popular social networks like Facebook or Twitter are used to both spread and debunk conspiracy theories. Moreover, they are increasingly becoming the new arena of political debate, whose users almost evenly share both inclusive and exclusionary messages.

Shifting to traditional media, data reveal that the use of television or newspapers as sources of information has a different impact on the three types of sovereignism. The frequent use of television would slightly discourage support for political sovereignist claims; on the other hand, it would encourage the exclusionary attitudes of those claims here reconducted to the cultural label. Finally, the use of television has no significant impact on economic sovereignism. The frequent use of newspapers seems to only influence attitudes towards cultural sovereignism, as it would likely drive people away from exclusionary attitudes. These findings reveal that those sectors of the population using a popular medium like television would be less attracted by claims that would undermine the status quo, namely the subversion of the traditional mechanisms of representative democracy; however, they would tend to be sensitive to messages related to the threats to a country's culture and identity. By contrast, the reflective thinking that is commonly associated with the habit of reading newspapers would encourage liberal and multicultural views.

Sovereignism as a channel of discontent?

Results only partially confirm hypothesis H2 on political inefficacy. The positive – and somewhat large – coefficient for external efficacy for all three dependent variables suggests that when people feel that their voices are unheard by politics and the political elite, they turn to critical positions against the traditional mechanisms of political representation (political sovereignism), against inclusionary models of a liberal and multicultural society (cultural sovereignism), and against supranational governance of the economy (economic sovereignism).

However, the variable measuring internal political efficacy works in the exact opposite way, although with a somewhat moderate magnitude coefficient, which is even not significant for economic sovereignism: thinking of politics as a not particularly complex thing increases people's willingness to restore full popular sovereignty. To explain this finding, we could observe that the success of sovereignist arguments relies on an increasingly diffuse perception that politics is less complicated than expected, and it does not require too much sophistication. A typical sovereignist argument is that even when possessing modest factual knowledge on complex issues, like the economy or global migration, ordinary citizens could be savvier than the ruling elite. So actually – the sovereignist claim runs – why do we need to pay for costly and unresponsive politicians in Brussels or in the obscure national parliaments, if the (sovereign) people could decide on their own?

The ideological side of sovereignism

Model estimates support the third hypothesis on ideology. Partisan cues[11] are a powerful predictor of sovereignist attitudes. Leaning towards a party promoting either political, cultural, or economic sovereignist claims, would increase support for sovereignist theses. Indeed, national political parties still retain a heuristic role in orienting people's attitudes on matters on which average citizens probably do not have sufficiently structured positions (Hooghe & Marks, 2005).

By controlling for left-right ideology, however, we must note that the effect of this predictor further emphasizes the theoretical distinction of sovereignism into three distinct dimensions.

On the one hand, results suggest an inverted U-shaped relationship between political and economic sovereignism and left-right ideology. Radical-left supporters stand out as more critical against the current mechanisms of representative democracy, followed by those of the radical right. They are also, critically, against the global economy, although to a lesser degree than radical and moderate right-wing voters, respectively. Moderate people leaning to the centre of the left-right spectrum would be less likely to share political-sovereignist or economic-sovereignist arguments.

On the other hand, the relationship between cultural sovereignism and ideology seems to be a linear one, as moving towards the right end of the continuum significantly increases people's willingness to raise the drawbridges of their own countries to other cultures and identities.

Sovereignist supporters in context

To conclude, all models control for the effect of people's socio-demographic background. Gender and age have a limited impact only on support for cultural sovereignism, with men more likely to endorse cultural-sovereignist claims than women. Looking at the age effect, data reveal that support for cultural and economic sovereignism slightly increases among the older age cohorts.

Higher levels of education tend to drive away people from the exclusionary attitudes of cultural sovereignism, as well as from the criticism of representative democracy within political sovereignism. By contrast, the impact of education on economic sovereignism almost disappears when introducing conspiracy thinking into the model and remains significant only for high levels of education: this finding suggests that conspiratorial beliefs are likely to fuel distrust and aversion against supranational economic elites and institutions, regardless of the level of education.

Finally, dummy variables for the surveyed countries suggest that a different exposure to global challenges like the financial or migration crisis, or national political turmoil, might make one country's population more sensitive to certain sovereignist arguments than others. For instance, political- sovereignist claims tend to be particularly popular in Greece, followed by the Czech Republic; they are also quite widespread across other southern countries like Italy, Spain and Portugal. Building walls and raising fences against migrants seems to be a preferred option among people living in the Czech Republic, a country that has adopted a hard position against the common EU policy on immigration. Finally, living in Greece, the country that suffered most from the consequences of the financial crisis, as well as the austerity measures imposed by Brussels, increases the likelihood of sharing the arguments of economic sovereignism, as compared to the other surveyed countries.

Concluding remarks

Sovereignism and populism are increasingly making headlines around the world, but their nature and definition still remains largely imprecise. Moreover, while literature has often treated the two concepts separately, they are increasingly associated in the current representations and narratives of political events.

In this paper, we have sought to single out sovereignism and populism as two distinct, yet interrelated concepts. In particular, we argued that sovereignism is one of the recurrent and core themes of populism, and pre-exists it; populism just took over ideas such as those of popular sovereignty and regains a decision-making power under a narrower, territorial authority – which often coincides, although not necessarily, with the national state. This means that there could be sovereignism without populism, but there is no populism that does not include sovereignist arguments in its, albeit 'thin' (Mudde, 2004), ideology.

Upon this distinction, we have provided a theoretical framework to conceive sovereignism as a multidimensional concept, onto a three-fold space defined by the nature of the 'sovereign people' addressed, namely as: ordinary citizens (political sovereignism), national people (cultural sovereignism), and state's people (economic sovereignism). They represented the dependent variables on which were tested the three hypotheses in support of sovereignist arguments.

Results showed that only some predictors are common to all three dimensions, and in particular, *conspiracy thinking*, *party-cueing*, and *political efficacy*. On the other hand, the use of media, left-right ideological orientations, and socio-demographic background do not have the same impact on the three dimensions. These results confirm the theoretical argument that sovereignism is intrinsically multidimensional, not only in the supply side, but also in the demand side.

The paper also shed a light onto the inextricable relationship between sovereignty and populism. By assuming that sovereignist claims are the core theme and the 'common denominator' (Kallis, 2018) of all populist movements, we argued that populist parties feed on sovereignist arguments, but also serve as 'issue entrepreneurs' (Hobolt & De Vries, 2015), by drawing the attention to the party system on sovereignty claims. Data revealed that populist movements are able to capitalize and manipulate people's discontent, by fostering sovereignist attitudes among their voters.

A more substantial implication of these findings is that, although populist parties emerged as a powerful catalyst of these attitudes, the intrinsic heterogeneity of the sovereignist supporters makes it difficult for one single movement to capitalize all three of the dimensions and mobilize voters on all of them. Another important insight, however, emerges from analyses concerning the impact of conspiracy thinking in fostering sovereignist theses. This should warn of the risk that future electoral campaigns will increasingly rely on media companies and political strategists, who are able to manipulate falsehoods and misleading news, and create virtual rallying spots for populist movements campaigning on sovereignist claims.

Notes

1. Social media users 'tend to form groups of like-minded people where they polarize their opinion' (Del Vicario et al., 2017), the so-called 'echo chambers', sharing only information that is likely to reinforce pre-existing beliefs.
2. These surveys are part of an EU-funded project, financed by the H2020 research and innovation programme, under grant agreement n. 649281 (www.euengage.eu)
3. Interviews were conducted using a Computer Assisted Web Interview (CAWI) method, with respondents approached through online panels. Quotas and weighting variables have been

used to limit self-selection bias due to online panels' non-probabilistic sampling procedures. Weighting variables are based on age, gender, region, education, and Internet usage, and are constructed using a rim-weighting procedure.

4. Both the 2016 and 2017 samples have been obtained by removing the 'speeders', that is, those respondents who took less than 50% of the median time to answer. Analyses were conducted on a sample of 11,140 respondents.

5. We opted for oblique rotation because we argue that factors might be correlated amongst them (Costello & Osborne, 2005; Kim & Mueller, 1978; Acock, 2014). However, we would obtain fairly similar results with an orthogonal rotation like varimax.

6. The full text of survey items is presented in the Appendix.

7. All items were rescaled into a 0–1 scale, with 0 indicating sovereignist attitudes, and 1 the opposite. Descriptives for the indexes are shown in the appendix. The summative index is then constructed by using standardized (mean 0, variance 1) values for the individual items.

8. The alpha would not vary by removing any of the three items. The relatively low alpha for this index can be explained by the lower number of items used to build this index (Acock, 2014; Cortina, 1993). As a rule of thumb, the advisable threshold for alpha is 0.70 (Nunnally, 1978; Peterson, 1994). For exploratory studies, however, alphas between 0.50 and 0.60 are considered adequate (King, 2009, p. 344; Nunnally, 1967). Moreover, the average inter-item correlation is 0.28, which is within the range recommended by Briggs and Cheek (1986, p. 114) of item homogeneity for a scale.

9. The items used as independent variables, with their descriptives, are shown in the Appendix.

10. The CHES 2017 has been produced as a part of the EUENGAGE project (www.chesdata.eu) .

11. The variable built by using the CHES-based index would include in the analysis only those people clearly expressing a party preference, and only among the parties analysed by CHES. This would reduce the sample of more than 2,000 units. To avoid this, we recoded the CHES-based variables by assigning the value 1 to those people feeling close to parties, scoring between −1 and −0.10 (obtained by combining: strongly sovereignist, scoring from −1 to −0.60, moderately sovereignist, scoring from −0.60 to −0.10) on the three populist indexes, and 0 if otherwise. We then ran the OLS models both with the continue variables and with the dummy variable. Since both models hold similar results, with magnitude of coefficients basically unvaried, we present the models using the dummy variable for party cueing.

Funding

This work was supported by H2020 Societal Challenges [grant number 649281].

ORCID

Linda Basile http://orcid.org/0000-0003-2842-1264

References

Abts, K., & Rummens, S. (2007). Populism versus democracy. *Political Studies, 55*(2), 405–424.

Acock, A. C. (2014). *A Gentle Introduction to Stata* (Fourth Edition). College Station, Texas: Stata Press.

Azrout, R., & de Vreese, C. (2018). The moderating role of identification and campaign exposure in party cueing effects. *West European Politics, 41*(2), 384–399.

Basile, L., & Mazzoleni, O. (2020). Sovereignist Wine in populist Bottles? An introduction. *European Politics and Society, 21*(2), 151–162.

Bessi, A., Coletto, M., Davidescu, G. A., Scala, A., Caldarelli, G., & Quattrociocchi, W. (2015). Science vs conspiracy: Collective narratives in the Age of Misinformation. *PLOS ONE, 10*(2), e0118093.

Brader, T., Tucker, J., & Duell, D. (2013). Which parties Can lead opinion? Experimental evidence in Partisan Cue taking in Multiparty Democracies. *Comparative Political Studies, 46*(11), 1485–1517.

Briggs, S. R., & Cheek, J. M. (1986). The role of factor analysis in the development and evaluation of personality scales. *Journal of Personality, 54*(1), 106–148.

Bullock, J. G. (2011). Elite influence on public opinion in an Informed Electorate. *American Political Science Review, 105*(3), 496–515.

Canovan, M. (1999). Trust the people! populism and the Two Faces of democracy. *Political Studies, 47* (1), 2–16.

Cortina, J. M. (1993). What is coefficient alpha? *An Examination of Theory and Applications. Journal of Applied Psychology, 78*(1), 98–104.

Costello, A. B., & Osborne, J. W. (2005). Best practices in Exploratory factor analysis: Four Recommendations for Getting the most from your analysis. *Practical Assessment, Research & Evaluation, 10*(7), 9.

Craig, S. C., & Maggiotto, M. A. (1982). Measuring political efficacy. *Political Methodology, 8*(3), 85–109.

Dalton, R. J., Beck, P., & Huckfeldt, R. (1998). Partisan cues and the media: Information Flows in the 1992 Presidential Election. *American Political Science Review, 92*(1), 111–126.

Del Vicario, M., Gaito, S., Quattrociocchi, W., Zignani, M., & Zollo, F. (2017). *Public discourse and news consumption on online social media: A quantitative, cross-platform analysis of the Italian Referendum* (Working Paper).

Flynn, D. J., Nyhan, B., & Reifler, J. (2017). The nature and Origins of Misperceptions: Understanding False and Unsupported beliefs about politics. *Political Psychology, 38*(S1), 127–150.

Goertzel, T. (1994). Belief in conspiracy theories. *Political Psychology, 15*(4), 731–742.

Hobolt, S. B., & De Vries, C. E. (2015). Issue entrepreneurship and Multiparty Competition. *Comparative Political Studies, 48*(9), 1159–1185.

Hooghe, L., & Marks, G. (2005). Calculation, community and cues: Public opinion on European integration. *European Union Politics, 6*(4), 419–443.

Kallis, A. (2018). Populism, Sovereigntism, and the Unlikely Re-emergence of the territorial nation-state. *Fudan Journal of the Humanities and Social Sciences, 11*(3), 285–302.

Kelly, D. (2017). Populism and the History of popular sovereignty. In C. R. Kaltwasser, P. Taggart, P. Ochoa Espejo, & P. Ostiguy (Eds.), *The Oxford Handbook of populism* (pp. 605–631). Oxford: Oxford University Press.

Kemmers, R. (2017). Channelling discontent? Non-voters, populist party voters, and their meaningful political agency. *European Journal of Cultural and Political Sociology, 4*(4), 381–406.

Kim, J.-O., & Mueller, C. W. (1978). *Factor analysis: Statistical methods and Practical issues.* Beverly Hills, CA: Sage.

King, W. R. (2009). *Knowledge Management and Organizational Learning.* London: Springer Science & Business Media.

Kriesi, H. (2014). The populist Challenge. *West European Politics, 37*(2), 361–378. doi:10.1080/01402382.2014.887879

Kriesi, H., Grande, E., Dolezal, M., Helbling, M., Höglinger, D., Hutter, S., & Wüest, B. (2012). *Political Conflict in Western Europe.* Cambridge: Cambridge University Press.

Magni, G. (2017). It's the Emotions, Stupid! Anger about the economic crisis, Low political efficacy, and support for populist parties. *Electoral Studies, 50*, 91–102.

Marks, G. (1999). Territorial identities in the European Union. In J. J. Anderson (Ed.), *Regional integration and democracy: Expanding on the European Experience* (pp. 69–91). Lanham, MD: Rowman & Littlefield.

McClosky, H., & Chong, D. (1985). Similarities and Differences between left-wing and right-wing Radicals. *British Journal of Political Science, 15*(03), 329–363.

Mény, Y., & Surel, Y. (2002). *Democracies and the populist Challenge.* New York: Palgrave Macmillan.

Miller, J. M., Saunders, K. L., & Farhart, C. E. (2016). Conspiracy endorsement as Motivated Reasoning: The Moderating Roles of political knowledge and trust. *American Journal of Political Science, 60*(4), 824–844. doi:10.1111/ajps.12234

Minkenberg, M. (2000). The Renewal of the radical right: Between Modernity and anti-modernity. *Government and Opposition, 35*(2), 170–188.

Mudde, C. (2004). The populist Zeitgeist. *Government and Opposition, 39*(4), 541–563.

Mudde, C. (2007). *Populist radical right parties in Europe* (1 edizione). Cambridge, UK; New York: Cambridge University Press.

Mudde, C. (2016). *The Study of Populist Radical Right Parties: Towards a Fourth Wave* (Working Paper No. 1) (pp. 1–23). Oslo: University of Oslo.

Mudde, C., & Kaltwasser, P. C. R. (2012). Populism and (liberal) democracy. In C. Mudde & C. R. Kaltwasser (Eds.), *Populism in Europe and the Americas: Threat or Corrective for democracy?* (pp. 1–26). Cambridge; New York: Cambridge University Press.

Nunnally, J. C. (1967). *Psychometric theory*. New York: McGraw-Hill.

Nunnally, J. C. (1978). *Psychometric theory*. New York: McGraw-Hill.

Oliver, J. E., & Wood, T. J. (2014). Conspiracy theories and the paranoid style(s) of mass opinion. *American Journal of Political Science, 58*(4), 952–966.

Peterson, R. A. (1994). A Meta-analysis of Cronbach's coefficient alpha. *Journal of Consumer Research, 21*(2), 381–391.

Polk, J., Rovny, J., Bakker, R., Edwards, E., Hooghe, L., Jolly, S., … Zilovic, M. (2017). Explaining the salience of anti-elitism and reducing political corruption for political parties in Europe with the 2014 Chapel Hill expert survey data. *Research & Politics, 4*(1), 1–9.

Rooduijn, M., van der Brug, W., & de Lange, S. L. (2016). Expressing or fuelling discontent? The relationship between populist voting and political discontent. *Electoral Studies, 43*, 32–40.

Sassen, S. (1996). *Losing control? Sovereignty in the Age of globalization*. New York: Columbia University Press.

Silva, B. C., Vegetti, F., & Littvay, L. (2017). The elite Is Up to something: Exploring the Relation between populism and belief in conspiracy theories. *Swiss Political Science Review, 23*(4), 423–443.

Spruyt, B., Keppens, G., & Van Droogenbroeck, F. (2016). Who supports populism and what Attracts people to It? *Political Research Quarterly, 69*(2), 335–346.

Sulitzeanu-Kenan, R., & Halperin, E. (2013). Making a Difference: Political efficacy and policy Preference construction. *British Journal of Political Science, 43*(2), 295–322.

Taggart, P. (2004). Populism and representative politics in contemporary Europe. *Journal of Political Ideologies, 9*(3), 269–288.

Wood, M. J., Douglas, K. M., & Sutton, R. M. (2012). Dead and Alive: Beliefs in Contradictory conspiracy theories. *Social Psychological and Personality Science, 3*(6), 767–773.

APPENDIX

Analyses conducted on a sample of N = 11,140.

Dependent variables: Political, Cultural, and Economic sovereignism

Descriptive analyses for variables used in Principal Factor Analysis

Table A1. Perception of migrants (% – weighted).

	%
'Can you please indicate to what extent you agree or disagree with the following statements about the general impact of immigration on [COUNTRY] and [NATIONALITY] people?' (Answer options: 1. Strongly agree, 2. Somewhat agree, 3. Somewhat disagree, 4. Strongly disagree). – % Strongly/somewhat agree	
Immigrants increase the likelihood of a *terrorist attack* in (OUR COUNTRY)	70
Immigrants *contribute more in taxes* than they benefit from health and welfare services mewhat disagree.	71
Immigration in general will *improve our culture* with new ideas and customs	56
The *religious practices* of immigrants are a threat to the (NATIONALITY) way of life and its traditions – % Strongly/ somewhat agree.	59
Immigrants are a significant cause of *crime* in (OUR COUNTRY).	59

SOVEREIGNISM AND POPULISM

Table A2. EU as a threat to nation (% – weighted).

'Some people say that the European Union might endanger some important aspects of the nation. For each of the following aspects, please indicate to what extent you agree or disagree that they are endangered by the European Union.' (Answer options: 1. Strongly agree, 2. Somewhat agree, 3. Somewhat disagree, 4. Strongly disagree). – % Strongly/somewhat agree.

	%
Achievements of the *welfare* system in [COUNTRY]	57
Economic growth in [COUNTRY]	59

Table A3. Satisfaction with the EU democracy (% – weighted).

'On the whole, how satisfied are you with how democracy works in the EU?' (Answer options: 1:Very dissatisfied, 2: somewhat dissatisfied, 3: somewhat satisfied, 4: very satisfied).

	%
% Very/somewhat dissatisfied.	62

Table A4. Trust in [Country] government (% – weighted).

'How much of the time do you think you can trust the [COUNTRY] government to do what is right?' (Answer options: 1. Never, 2. Only some of the time, 3. Most of the time, 4. Just about always).

	%
% Never/Only some of the time.	75

Table A5. Effects of globalization (weighted).

'Do you think that, overall, globalisation has a positive or negative effect on [Nationality] citizens?'

	Mean	Standard deviation	Median	Min.	Max.
0 = Globalization has a negative effect; 10 = Globalization has a positive effect	4.7	2.4	5	0	10

Table A6. Preferences for direct vs. representative democracy (weighted).

'Which number from 0 to 10 best represents how you think the system of governing Europe should work?'

	Mean	Standard deviation	Median	Min.	Max.
0 = Ordinary people making all decisions on their own; 10 = Elected politicians and officials making all decisions on their own	5	2.2	5	0	10

Table A7. Supranational vs. National authority on policy issues (weighted).

'For each of the following policy alternatives, please position yourself on a scale from 0 to 10. If your views are somewhere in between, you can choose any number that best describes your decision.'

	Mean	Standard deviation	Median	Min.	Max.
(Migration): 0 = [COUNTRY] should decide for itself how many immigrants to accept each year; 10 = The EU should decide how many immigrants should be accepted by each Member State each year.	3.7	3.2	4	0	10
(Economy): 0 = Retaining full powers for economic decision making; 10 = Giving the EU more authority over Member States' economic and budgetary policies	3.7	2.4	4	0	10

SOVEREIGNISM AND POPULISM

Table A8. Indexes of Sovereignist claims.

	Mean	Standard deviation	Median	Min.	Max.
Political sovereignism	0.41	0.18	0.42	0	1
Cultural sovereignism	0.39	0.24	0.39	0	1
Economic sovereignism	0.43	0.20	0.29	0	1

Independent variables

Table A9. Items used for conspiracy index (% – weighted).

'To what extent you agree or disagree with each of the following statements?' (Answer options: 1. Strongly agree, 2. Somewhat agree, 3. Somewhat disagree, 4. Strongly disagree). – % Strongly/somewhat agree

	%
We would be much better off now if our foreign affairs were conducted out in the open, for all to see, rather than secretly.	76
Most of the news we get from the press and the radio is deliberately slanted to mislead us.	69
I often feel that the really important matters are decided behind the scenes, by people we never even hear about	82
The people think they govern themselves, but they really don't[a].	74
A secretive power elite with a globalist agenda is conspiring to eventually rule the world through an authoritarian world government, or New World Order.	47
Actually, it is not the government that runs the country: we don't know who pulls the strings.	58
Some people say officials of the European Union are gradually seeking to take over all law-making powers in this country.	56
The US administration of President Trump/ Russian administration of President Putin is behind the migrant crisis because it is in its interest to create chaos in Europe and split the Union's 28 member states over the issue.	41
The [NATIONALITY] government/EU institution is deliberately hiding the truth about how many immigrants really live in this country	63

[a]The first four items come from McClosky and Chong's battery of items (1985) to assess people's paranoid tendencies.

Table A10. Conspiracy index (weighted).

9 items' scale – Cronbach's alpha = 0.85					
	Mean	Standard deviation	Median	Min.	Max.
0 = High conspiracy thinking 1 = Low conspiracy thinking.	0.4	0.2	0.4	0	1

Table A11. Frequency of use of media (weighted).

'Roughly how many times a week do you normally do the following activities?' (Answer options: 1: Never; 2: Less than once a week; 3: Once a week; 4: 2 times a week; 5: 3 times a week; 6: 4 times a week; 7: 5 times a week; 8: 6 times a week; 9: Every day) – rescaled into a 0–1 scale.

	Mean	Standard deviation	Median	Min.	Max.
Listening to or watching the news about politics and society on TV.	0.6	0.4	0.8	0	1
Reading about politics and society in a newspaper.	0.4	0.4	0.3	0	1
Listening to or watching the news about politics and society on social media (Facebook, Twitter, etc.).	0.5	0.4	0.4	0	1

Table A12. External and internal political efficacy (% – weighted).

'You find below a list of some opinions on politics that people sometimes express. To what extent you agree or disagree with each of them?' (Answer options: 1. Strongly agree; 2. Somewhat agree; 3. Somewhat disagree; 4 Strongly disagree) -% Strongly agree/Agree

	%
People like me have no influence on what the government does	75
Politicians don't really care what people like me think	85
Sometimes politics is so complicated that I cannot understand what is really happening.	61

SOVEREIGNISM AND POPULISM

Table A13. External efficacy (weighted).

2 items' scale – Cronbach's alpha = 0.69 (Influence on what the government does; Politicians don't really care).

	Mean	Standard deviation	Median	Min.	Max.
0 = Low efficacy; 1 = High efficacy.	0.3	0.2	0.3	0	1

Table A14. Party cueing – based on CHES data.

	Mean	St. dev.	Median	Min.	Max.
People vs. elite = position on direct vs. representative democracy. Some political parties take the position that 'the people' should have the final say on the most important issues, for example, by voting directly in referendums. At the opposite pole are political parties that believe that elected representatives should make the most important political decisions.					
People vs. elite (Position): 0'The people', not politicians, should make the most important decisions; 10 = Elected office holders should make the most important decisions	5.00	2.26 2.26	4.43	0.79	9.80
Salience of **anti-establishment and anti-elite rhetoric**: 0 = Not important at all; 10 = Extremely important	4.79	2.79	4.35	0.75	10.00
Party cueing: Salience*(Position-Mean Country Position)	*0.49*	*0.36*	*0.61*	*−1.00*	*1.00*
Immigrate policy = position on immigration policy (0 = Fully in favour of a restrictive policy on immigration; 10 = Fully opposed to a restrictive policy on immigration)	5.90	2.75	5.94	0.67	9.91
Multiculture = position on integration of immigrants and asylum seekers (multiculturalism vs. assimilation): 0 = Strongly favours assimilation; 10 = Strongly favours multiculturalism	5.93	2.66	6.00	1.39	9.95
Immigrate salience (importance/salience of immigration policy): 0 = No importance; 10 = Great importance	5.85	1.85	5.64	1.62	10.00
Multiculture salience (importance/salience of integration policy for immigrants and asylum seekers): 0 = No importance 10 = Great importance	5.90	1.78	5.70	2.64	9.92
Cultural sovereignist claims (Cronbach's alpha 0.97)	*0.12*	*0.59*	*0.09*	*−0.91*	*1.00*
Party cueing: Salience*(Position-Mean Country Position) – rescaled	*0.19*	*0.41*	*0.25*	*−0.74*	*1.00*
EU position (overall orientation of the party leadership towards European integration): 1 = Strongly opposed; 2 = opposed; 3 = somewhat opposed; 4 = Neutral; 5 = somewhat in favour; 6 = in favour; 7 = strongly in favour	4.66	1.90	5.11	1.05	7.00
EU budget (position of the party leadership on EU authority over member states' economic and budgetary policies): 1 = Strongly opposes; 7 = strongly favours	3.51	1.62	3.70	1.00	6.30
EU salience (relative salience of European integration in the party's public stance): 0 = European Integration is of no importance, never mentioned 10 = European Integration is the most important issue.	6.34	1.42	6.29	3.38	9.86
Economic sovereignist claims (Cronbach's alpha = 0.96)	*0.09*	*0.62*	*0.20*	*−1.00*	*1.00*
Party cueing: Salience*(Position-Mean Country Position)	*0.11*	*0.46*	*0.17*	*−1.00*	*1.00*

106 SOVEREIGNISM AND POPULISM

Table A15. Party cueing – based on CHES data: parties scoring <−0.10 on CHES-based indexes (−1; +1 scale).

Party name	Abbreviation	Country
Political sovereignism		
Svoboda a přímá demokracie – Tomio Okamura	SPD	Czech Republic
Front National	FN	France
La France Insoumise	LFI	France
Movimento 5 Stelle	M5S	Italy
Lega	Lega	Italy
Partij voor de Vrijheid	PVV	The Netherlands
Forum voor Democratie	FVD	The Netherlands
Kukiz' 15	Kukiz'15	Poland
Podemos	Podemos	Spain
Cultural sovereignism		
Svoboda a přímá demokracie – Tomio Okamura	SPD	Czech Republic
Komunistická strana Čech a Moravy	KSCM	Czech Republic
Les Républicains (formerly UMP)	LR	France
Front National	FN	France
Debout la France	DLF	France
Alternative für Deutschland	AfD	Germany
Christlich-Soziale Union in Bayern	CSU	Germany
Nea Dimokratia	ND	Greece
Khrisi Avgi	XA	Greece
Anexartitoi Ellines	ANEL	Greece
Enosi Kentroon	EK	Greece
Fratelli d'Italia	FdI	Italy
Lega	Lega	Italy
Forza Italia	FI	Italy
Partij voor de Vrijheid	PVV	The Netherlands
Volkspartij voor Vrijheid en Democratie	VVD	The Netherlands
Staatkundig Gereformeerde Partij	SGP	The Netherlands
Christen Democratisch Appèl	CDA	The Netherlands
Forum voor Democratie	FVD	The Netherlands
Prawo i Sprawiedliwość	PiS	Poland
Kukiz' 15	Kukiz'15	Poland
Korwin/Wolnosc	Wolnosc	Poland
Centro Democrático Social	CDS-PP	Portugal
Partido Popular Democrático/Partido Social Democrata	PSD	Portugal
Partido Popular	PP	Spain
Ciudadanos Partido de la Ciudadania	C's	Spain
Coalicion Canaria	CC	Spain
Conservative and Unionist Party	C	United Kingdom
Democratic Unionist Party	DUP	United Kingdom
UK Independence Party	UKIP	United Kingdom
Economic sovereignism		
Svoboda a přímá demokracie – Tomio Okamura	SPD	Czech Republic
Komunistická strana Čech a Moravy	KSCM	Czech Republic
Občanská Demokratická Strana	ODS	Czech Republic
La France Insoumise	LFI	France
Parti Commuiste Française	PCF	France
Front National	FN	France
Debout la France	DLF	France
Alternative für Deutschland	AfD	Germany
Nea Dimokratia	ND	Greece
Khrisi Avgi	XA	Greece
Anexartitoi Ellines	ANEL	Greece
Movimento 5 Stelle	M5S	Italy
Fratelli d'Italia	FdI	Italy
Lega	Lega	Italy
Partij voor de Vrijheid	PVV	The Netherlands
Socialistische Partij	SP	The Netherlands
Forum voor Democratie	FVD	The Netherlands
Prawo i Sprawiedliwość	PiS	Poland

(*Continued*)

Table A15. Continued.

Party name	Abbreviation	Country
Kukiz' 15	Kukiz'15	Poland
Korwin/Wolnosc	Wolnosc	Poland
Bloco de Esquerda	BE/O Bloco	Portugal
Podemos	Podemos	Spain
Izquierda Unida – Unidad Popular	IU	Spain
Euskal Herria Bildu	EA/EH Bildu	Spain
Conservative and Unionist Party	C	United Kingdom
Democratic Unionist Party	DUP	United Kingdom
UK Independence Party	UKIP	United Kingdom
Labour	Lab	United Kingdom

Conclusions. The populism-sovereignism linkage: findings, theoretical implications and a new research agenda

Luca Verzichelli 🆔

ABSTRACT
In this article, an assessment of the sovereignism- populism linkage is offered, moving from the main findings emerged in the contributions to this special issue. The sovereignism- populism linkage is seen as a challenge for comparative politics: on the one hand, the copious literature already developed, particularly in the specific field of populist parties, offers a broad set of findings and stimuli. On the other hand, the huge application (and the abuse) of the concept of populism, which has been associated to a number of very different phenomena, make the discussion on its relationships with cognate concepts more and more difficult. The article offers a first attempt to review the knowledge on the sovereignism-populism linkage, defining a new space for the empirical analysis, and refreshing the research agenda, in particular regarding some classical themes in comparative politics like the 'sustainability' of political elites and the crisis of representative institutions.

1. The populism-sovereignism linkage as a new challenge

As pointed out in the introduction to this special issue, the linkage between *sovereignism* and *populism* has not been, so far, sufficiently explored by the comparative analyses of current political change. As Basile and Mazzoleni suggest (Introduction in this issue), in the past, the two concepts at the core of this study have been developed along two separate paths, discussed by different communities of scholars, with rather different goals. Indeed, those who have, at length, been engaged with the notion of sovereignty – mainly lawyers – have tended to stress the normative meaning of the concept, in terms of more or less pronounced inclusiveness of the *people,* that is in the end the bearer of the traditional liberal idea of national sovereignty. On the other hand, political scientists and historians have been more interested in the notion of populism, with increasing interest in the recent decades, in order to stress the increasing demand for a 'non-mediated' and popular spirit of democratic politics, based on a strong anti-elitist sentiment.

Notwithstanding the differentiation between the two concepts, however, the contributions included in the present special issue show that a reflection on the linkage between the recent developments of the idea of sovereignism and the wide literature on populism seems particularly fruitful today. Indeed, all the articles share the idea that those actors labelled as 'populist' could be analyzed by looking at their positions on territorial authority, national sovereignty or 'people's sovereignty'. In carrying out those undertakings, they demonstrate that the increasingly evident variability of the populist appeals actually corresponds to a plurality of claims for sovereignty.

These articles represent a major advancement for the research agenda, as they explore the linkage between populism and sovereignism from different analytical perspectives. In particular, they look both at the demand-side and to the supply-side perspective of political change. On the one hand, we can easily associate the emergence of several cases of elites or leaders' discourse appealing to the 'true people' and denouncing the damages produced by globalization, Europeanism and elitism, in terms of a loss of sovereignty. On the other hand, these articles present the evidence of a number of 'bottom up' demands dealing with the typical conditions of sovereignty: public opinion and the electorates, all around Europe, would be asking for more national independence, more secure national borders and more attention to national (or traditional) cultures. The growing demand of sovereignty has been developed by a number of voters/citizens who seem now ready to change their long-lasting political preferences, and to give a chance to some new vocal populist actors, whose main pledge is to 'clean' the political scene from these unproductive political elites, thus bringing the democratic mechanisms back to the 'people'.

Overall, the articles support the argument that the current applications of populism and the growing demand for sovereignism are necessarily connected: as Basile and Mazzoleni argue, 'sovereignism is one of the recurrent, and core, themes of populism. Sovereignty claims pre-exists populism' (introduction in this issue). Although the linkage between the two concepts is strong and evident, however, the nature of such relationship looks, now more than ever, slippery and complicated. Indeed, we could agree that the populist thin-ideology of the stereotypical European 'far-right' or 'nationalistic' parties is somehow imbued with sovereigntist arguments, but the *populist style* of many other political actors may take those arguments to a much lesser extent.

Furthermore, we may conceive quite a few forms and aspects of sovereignism – that is to say expressions and expectations emphasizing the importance of a univocal and national sovereignty – in a number of traditional political actors who are not currently labelled as populists: ' ... there could be sovereignism without populism, but there is no populist discourse that does not include sovereigntist arguments' (Ibid.). In other words, a fully-fledged populist discourse emerges only when a plurality of aspects of sovereignism are recalled, while a single manifestation of sovereignism cannot be considered a sufficient condition to talk about populism.

The contributions, by working on different units of analysis, and employing a rather wide set of methodological instruments, basically agree on the necessity to distinguish (at least) three dimensions of sovereignism: a cultural one, dealing with the need to preserve national, ethnic, linguistic and religious identities; a political dimension, connected to the defence of people's sovereignty from the endemic corruption produced by the elites; and an economic dimension, mainly dealing with the protection of *our* prosperity from the demand of solidarity growing from the *others*.

These diverse dimensions and degrees of sovereignism look differently correlated to the different meanings of the concept of populism: from a still limited and mainly descriptive sample of studies, we can detect, for instance, that the aspect of populism often defined as a *communication style* (Moffit, 2016) is probably less related to the return of strong sovereigntist stances. More relevant, according to the findings discussed here, is the connection between sovereignism and that aspect of populism defined as a successful *political strategy* (Urbinati, 1998). And, of course, the linkage between sovereignism and the idea of populism as a soft ideological structure (Abts & Rummens, 2007; Mudde, 2007; 2016) is even stronger, since in such vision of populism, both the cultural, the political and the economic dimensions of sovereignism are crucial.

Of course, the researches presented here cannot cover the totality of messages conveyed today by an increasingly compound and variegated set of 'populist actors'. A comprehensive cognitive map of the connections defining the sovereignism-populism linkage is therefore yet to come. However, we can contend that the empirical space of application of any populist discourse can be shaped by different types of sovereigntist claims. That is *per se* a good point of departure, that I must say, until now, has not been sufficiently discussed by the scholars of empirical comparative politics.

In this contribution, I therefore aim to produce a first systematic assessment of this conceptual linkage. In the next sections, I will go back to some of the findings produced by the articles included in this special issue, to describe the extent and the scope of such an empirical space of application of the populist arguments in the contemporary scenario of democratic change. Looking at the linkage between populism and sovereignism, I will then try to define the sovereignism-populism linkage as a new research challenge for scholars of comparative politics, nowadays. This will be done by discussing the main implications these readings bring to scholars interested in the comparative analysis of political change.

The final section provides a further insight for future research, enouncing some preliminary propositions on the populism-sovereignism linkage. What I am going to propose here is a scheme, still sketchy, to respond to the question raised by the editors of this special issue about the need to develop a new research agenda on populism, exploring its linkages with sovereignism. And, at the same time provide a constructive suggestion, to make this research agenda more concrete and innovative. That is to say, a first proposal to build a new agenda connected to the appealing theme of populism, but in harmony with the evergreen subjects of comparative politics and in 'concert' with findings produced by a broader community of scholars, who want to understand and explain the true spirit of the current political changes.

2. Selected findings

A first interesting piece of evidence concerning the evolution of the populism-sovereignism linkage comes from the analysis of the Austrian case conducted by Heinisch, Werner and Habersack in their article. Indeed, the far-right populist party in this country (FPO) has remained relatively isolated for a long time in the Austrian party system. With the passing of time, however, the voters of the traditional mainstream conservative party (OVP) have assumed some more radical positions that are more and more similar to those expressed by the 'populists'. As a result, the approach, the style and, in the end, the coalition strategies of the new OVP leader, Sebastian Kurz, have changed, since the formation of his new government at the end of 2017, after the long process of coalition building, that has brought the far-right FPO back into the executive. By employing an intensive comparison of the manifestos of the two parties, and then analyzing survey data about the positioning of the voters during the past decade, the article captures the dynamics of change in the reconstruction of the sovereigntist claims in three specific domains: national, economic, and popular sovereignty. This allows the authors to produce a robust explanation of the recent evolutions of both a paradigmatic example of a 'far-right populist' European party and a 'mainstream-conservative' one.

A rather asymmetric and somehow ground-breaking process of party transformation has also occurred in the British case. Here, the profile of the main parties, more or less 'exposed' to an increasing demand of sovereignism, has been challenged by the insurgence of the Brexit issue. In their article, Baldini, Bressanelli and Gianfreda develop an interesting analysis of British MPs' parliamentary speeches between 2015 and 2017: the main evidence explored by this article concerns the emergence of a rather contrasting trend of sovereigntist claims in both the two mainstream parties. Indeed, while the *nationalist* claim seems to emerge among the Tory MPs – and particularly among the *Brexiters* from the Conservative group at the Commons – who also show the consolidation of some anti-elitist arguments, the Labour MPs tend to increase their attitudes towards *civic sovereignism,* thus stressing the importance of representative democracy at the domestic level, and the 'perils' of a too binding process of European integration.

The article by Mueller and Heidelberger moves to a different case – Switzerland – and to a different unit of analysis: the development of political, economic, and cultural sovereignism expressed by the voters by exercising their democratic right of direct participation to the legislation, over more than thirty years of referenda. The study offers a persuading picture of the impact of these three different sovereigntist arguments, but it also shows that the conflict between demarcation and integration and party preferences are increasingly more relevant in explaining the emergence of new individual positions on sovereignism. Hence, the Swiss case demonstrates that some of the sovereigntist and anti-integrationist values diffused among the citizens have been absorbed by the party polarization, even in the peculiar case of European (but not EU) consensus democracy.

In this respect, the analysis of the case of the Swiss People's party (SVP) provides an interesting transformation of a typical European 'populist actor' out of the EU context. This is what Ivaldi and Mazzoleni do in their article. The goal of the authors is, more precisely, to analyze the political supply, provided by a bunch of established European far-right populist parties and to produce an in-depth qualitative analysis of five relevant cases (the Austrian FPO, the French RN, the already mentioned Swiss SVP, the British UKIP and the Italian Lega). The research is based on the content of the party manifestos published during the post-crisis period. The main implication of this study is the increase of relevance of economic populist sovereignism, which seems to be a common feature in the recent transformation of all the parties belonging to this 'family' of political actors. This finding is particularly interesting, if one thinks that such a convergence among far-right parties is tested, despite the relatively high degree of variance they show when one looks to other aspects of the political discourse, including the typical socio-economic issues, between neo-liberal and protectionist stances.

Another extensive comparison included in the special issue is produced by Basile, Borri, and Verzichelli, whose article explores the sovereignism-populism linkage by analyzing the data from recent public opinion surveys. Findings show a distribution of public's attitudes along three dimensions of sovereignism: cultural, political and economic sovereignism, which are clearly distinguishable, looking at the attitudes of public opinion. Moreover, the article also offers an interpretative analysis which confirms three general hypotheses on the relevance of three *explananda which have* recently emerged in the literature: the conspiracy arguments, the perception of political efficacy, and party cueing. This means, according to the authors, that populist parties and leaders still have the chance to foster a range of different sovereigntist attitudes among the citizens. This corroborates their role of 'issue entrepreneurs' (Hobolt & de Vries, 2015) and also their potential for manipulation of those voters who show paranoid and conspirationist attitudes.

Although many other findings produced by the articles would deserve attention, I would like to focus my attention on the red line running through some of these pieces of evidence: as said, all the contributions of this special issue seem to indicate the compound nature of sovereignism and, at the same time, the presence of multidimensional attitudes in many – if not all – the European polities covered by the research. In other words, it is true that the heterogeneity of the sovereigntist arguments makes the possibility of finding an actor who supports and nurtures all of them, very unlikely. At the same time, the actors – parties and leaders – defined as 'populist' by the literature tend to chaotically mix up some of these arguments, and to manipulate them, involving public opinion in an intricate game of mutual influence. Such a complicated game determines a number of important implications for the dynamics of change in the overall public opinion as well as in the parties and party systems, determining relevant alterations in terms of leadership styles, political communication, policy priorities and coalition strategies. Notwithstanding the variety of the approaches used, all the articles in this special issue produce stimulating food for thought: we can use them to produce, at first, a comprehensive 'inventory' of the different meanings of sovereignism, and to connect these different demands to specific phenomena, to be then investigated by employing some specific indicators. In the next section, I will therefore move to a tentative systematic analysis of the theoretical implications generated by the growing demand of sovereignism in European democracies.

3. From empirical evidence to theoretical implications

A huge literature has been recently produced, in the effort to generate a systematic analysis of the relationships between populism and its cognate concepts. A few important contributions, for instance those by Mueller (2016) or Mudde and Rovira Kaltwasser (2012) are often indicated as the most valuable references to extract a few robust conceptual distinctions. However, the complexity of the conceptual muddle around the idea of populism is still evident, as three very different handbooks, recently produced, clearly shows (de la Torre, 2019; Heinisch, Holtz-Bacha, & Mazzoleni, 2017; Rovira Kaltwasser, Taggart, Ochoa Espejo, & Ostiguy, 2017). Moreover, as recently argued by Rooduijn (2019), the widening of the research agenda on an 'appealing' subject like populism has actually complicated our work due to fickleness of its application to several and different empirical targets. Accordingly, a lot of work is still needed in order to reach a comprehensive interpretation of such a compound phenomenon. A closer look at the multidimensional nature of populism, and in particular to the specific aspects that can be associated to different dimensions of sovereignism, seems to be very promising – and somehow necessary – work.

Indeed, the sovereignism-populism linkage is not new in literature, and it has already been considered in a few previous works (De Spiegeleire, Skinner, & Sweijs, 2017; Kallis,

2018). However, the theoretical and empirical research has not sufficiently developed the implications of such a distinction. It is therefore worth repeating such an argument after the reading of this collection of studies. Altogether, the articles I have briefly reviewed above confirm that the study of the linkage populism-sovereignism can help us to reduce the complexity of the first notion and, consequently, to define a sort of common denominator of the general concept of *populism* (Kallis, 2018). More precisely, a set of different dimensions of sovereignism can be fruitfully detected, in the attempt to find a more precise measure of the distances existing from one populist message to another. In the end, this empirical exercise will allow us to fix the 'borders' of the semantic perimeter of the concept of populism. That is to say, discovering the difference between a system of sovereigntist claims/indications/attitudes that, all together, design a clearly populist discourse, and a specific recall to any form of sovereignty, which *per se* cannot be labelled as a populist discourse.

As Basile and Mazzoleni highlight, the need to clearly define the semantic overlap between sovereignism and populism is a fundamental action we have to take in order to provide a more comprehensive and pragmatic theoretical framework to the understanding of populism. In the end, this action consists of both the challenges indicated by Rooduijn (2019, pp. 4–6) to overcome the ambiguity of the research produced so far: to avoid confusing populism with related concepts and to avoid keeping the research on populism attached to the result of the adjacent fields. Indeed, all the contributors in this special issue elaborate on the different empirical meanings of the two concepts and, at the same time, they define what aspects of sovereignism have to be considered crucial for the emergence of a number of populist experiences.

Therefore, the pieces of research we are assembling respond positively to the challenge, bringing a significant, although still limited, set of empirical examples concerning the different types of sovereigntist claims that can be associated to (or distinguished by) the populist experience. Thanks to these examples, we can draw a first series of theoretical implications based on the notion and on the multifaceted nature of sovereignism, to be adequately refined and completed at a later stage. Let us sketch out these implications in four points.

3.1. Sovereignism and national interests. Defence or counter-attack?

Undoubtedly, sovereignism is currently having an unprecedented relevance in many European realities, reframing of the notion of 'national interest' and, more in general, revitalizing the notion of 'nation'. A large part of this impact can be certainly absorbed by the return of a traditional idea of nationalism supported by the far-right populist parties (Mudde, 2007; Pirro, 2014; Van Kessel, 2015). However, to break the population of populist actors in two, on the basis of their attachment to the classical idea of nation, is far from being an easy task. We know already, for instance, that while nativist ideology and the authoritarian sense of a (national) state go together with the discourse of many populist far-right parties (Mudde, 2004), other nationalist claims are associated with the protection of specific cultural concerns.

The rise of anti-EU sovereignism is evidence of the multifaceted aims of these types of claims: the family of *Eurosceptic parties* has always been highly heterogeneous (Taggart & Szczerbiak, 2004). Even today, this family includes an assorted number of actors whose claims vary from the demand for 'protection' of some national specificities (the defensive approach of the *soft-Eurosceptic* parties), to an open critique of the process of integration from those who radically contest the process of the construction of the European Union. The differences in the supply-side shown by contemporary political actors are evident in the left-right dimension, but there are significant variations even within each ideological area (Pirro, Taggart, & van Kessel, 2018).

Therefore, we should be able to evaluate the true goal of the claim for a national sovereignty. By unpacking this dimension in a more or less sophisticated way, as proposed in some of the articles included in this special issue, it should be possible to get a more realistic, empirical oversight of the different definitions of national interest.

3.2. Sovereignism and domestic cultures. 'Enemies', 'others' and similar obsession effects

We should then consider the recent evolution of the sovereigntist discourse in the perspective of the establishment of a new style of leadership inspired by the celebration of a set of (national or traditional) cultural values, against the values of partisan ideologies. The affirmation 'our people first', very much used by several political leaders, mainly in the far-right camp, often looks like the attempt to preserve the consensus from those parts of the society whose reactions to globalism and Europeanism have basically determined a cultural bias against untreatable and unknown communities made up of 'others'. The construction of a new sense of sovereignism based on the obsession of the 'enemy' shows significant elements of similarity developed in rather different contexts. Undoubtedly, many right-wing populist parties and leaders – some of them studied in this special issue – have associated such a sense of sovereignism to the need to subvert the corruption of the elites by, bringing the power back to the people. However, milder messages of cultural sovereignism have been found in the discourse of a broader population of political actors who claim the necessities of 'our people', lamenting the excessive attention paid to the 'others'.

We can find the traces of some sort of cultural sovereignism in some of the findings achieved in the studies of this special issue covering different political actors and levels of analysis. For instance, the attempt to intercept the consensus of public opinion in defending the prerogatives of domestic way of life in Switzerland, or the political justification for the Brexit option developed by some conservative politicians in their public discourse. All these stories follow the same pattern of *filling the public-elites divide,* using the argument of the protection of a cultural sense of sovereignism. However, the narrative of 'othering' generates very different effects on the basis of the degree of cultural involvement, as showed by the anguished processes of change in many traditional party elites and electorates. The drift toward a populist discourse based on the defence of domestic cultures is not clear and not irreversible. An extensive empirical assessment, developing some of the suggestions from the articles presented here, is therefore needed.

3.3. Sovereignism and representative elites. Towards a personalized illiberal democracy?

We have then to focus on the claims for some kind of sovereignism produced by the strata of the society that are disenchanted and sceptical about the functioning of representative democracy. Of course, we tend to define as 'populist' those leaders who try to intercept these volatile and anti-elitist sentiments diffused through contemporary societies. But we should clarify the width and the real target of their contentions: to what extent can the new leaders use the arguments of elite corruption and ineffectiveness of democratic legislatures, by personalizing the leading of governmental institutions and the styles of policy making? Are they interested to increase the leadership room of manoeuvre to promote more functional packages of democratic policy alternatives, ore they just want to manipulate the basic rules of representative democracy to consolidate their personal power over the legislative and executive arenas?

This dimension of variability recalls the *responsibility vs. responsiveness* argument developed by Peter Mair (2014): the leaders entirely committed to their responsiveness would take benefit of their growing consensus to undermine the rules of democratic representation, while those who recall the necessity of a balance between responsiveness and responsibility (Flinders & Judge, 2017) would not fall into the temptation to exploit the argument of political sovereignism – *let's give the power back to our sovereign people* – to cultivate their personal power.

An even more sophisticated distinction can be done among those non pluralist and unaccountable forms of political representation which seem to emerge in times of crisis of political representation (Tormey, 2015). Following Caramani (2017), we can define two opposite forms of unaccountable representation: technocracy and populism. Indeed, both technocratic and populist leaders would challenge the traditional mechanisms of democratic representation, insisting on the predominance of the 'general interest' over 'politics as usual'. However, while the first notion stresses responsibility and conceives the need of a popular capability to respect the expertise of technocratic decision makers, the latter stresses responsiveness and requires a delegation to leaders who equate the general interest with a putative will of the people.

Following on this line of reasoning, we can argue that those actors who keep showing a total disinterest for responsibility, maximizing their responsiveness, are populist and charismatic leaders who stress the argument of political sovereignism, since they simply want to remove all kinds of constraints to their personal leadership. They demand national sovereignty, but they also need strong governmental powers and personalized parties that are supposed to die (or in any case to be dramatically downsized) after the end of their leadership.

In other words, an uncontrolled dose of sovereignism, combined with personal power, creates conditions of that form of *illiberal democracy* (Zakaria, 2007) which is not only a risk for unstable and hybrid regimes. The example of Hungary has been recently analyzed at length due to the duration and the cruelty of its current government, therefore someone already speaks of the *Orbanization* of the whole Hungarian political culture (Wilkin, 2018), but other leaders, recently emerged, tend to remove the external and moral constraints, mixing elements of national sovereignty with the idea of a full responsiveness. An example is provided by the leadership of Jaroslaw Kaczyńsk whose party – law and Justice – is still the leading actor of the Polish political system. But new leader of the Italian League, Matteo Salvini can be also assimilated to this category, when he insists, in his harsh critique of Brussels, on the loss of legitimacy of the leadership of EU office holders (with no difference between technocrats and political personalities).

On the other hand, we know that charisma and personalization are not just a matter for illiberal and electoral democracies, since the risk of a verticalization of political consent nurtured by simplification and polarization is everywhere in the democratic hemisphere (Urbinati, 2014). Indeed, we can argue that some of the recently emerged leaders, thanks to the wave of political mistrust and anti-party sentiment, may try to *disfigure* the democratic spirit, to build on the expression by Nadia Urbinati. Others, conversely, may use the arguments of sovereignism and the perspective of a simplification of representative democracies just for their purposes of limiting the effects of globalization and of supranational integration. But their action can be dangerous for the stability of the mechanisms of democratic mediation. The presence of the leaders of some populist movements/parties in government – the most relevant case is now probably that of the *Five Star Movement* in Italy should be studied in-depth to understand what conditions are necessary to establish a new equilibrium between personalization and liberal democracy.

A further implication concerning the relationship between sovereignism and representative democracy is the problem of 'elite sustainability' (Verzichelli, 2018a). To what extent can the European parliamentary democracies resist continuous electoral shifts and an uncontrolled turnover of their national political elites? The return to some 'ordinary' rate of elite circulation (Verzichelli, 2018b) is necessary to stabilize a system of responsible rulers and to crystallize the format of new party systems. In this respect, some sovereigntist arguments can be used to re-establish the prominence of 'domestic' representative democracy, as many MPs from Jeremy Corbyns' Labour have recently done. On the other hand, a purely Manichean and anti-elitist position would bring the truly populist leaders to promote platoons of 'personal soldiers' with no particular skill or peculiar kinds of advocacy, to occupy the key representative and ministerial positions.

3.4. Sovereignism and the redefinition of domestic economic policies. Regulation or a new protectionist paradigm?

Finally, I would like to consider another aspect of sovereignism which has proved to be very relevant in many of the contributions included in this special issue: the consolidation of the dissident views concerning the effects of the global economic order; if not an explicit rejection of it then inspiring the demand for a new set of economic measures. Again, we are certainly not opening a new bottle here: after all, the claims in favour of a popular opposition to the intrigues of global economy, financial elites and international capitalism are well known, originating during the course of the XIX century, as the root of *producerism*.

However, the wine offered today by many populist actors tastes very different in comparison to the times when the appeals to protect the domestic economic actors against the 'others', was actually limited to some provocative arguments – for instance the idea of special tariffs, or the launch of other protectionist policies balancing the openness of neo-liberal economies. Still in the mid-nineties of the XX century, when an isolated actor like Ross Perot was able to reach a significant consensus in the US, the demand for an economic sovereignism was not yet so evident.

Today, several economic issues are used in many 'neo-sovereigntist' appeals in Europe: from the new left to the extreme right, many actors explicitly mention the need to protect 'our economy', the 'made in ... .', and the conditions of 'our working class'. However, even in this case we must use a cautious approach. In particular, we should distinguish those protective claims which are not renouncing forms of solidarity towards other polities (especially within the same supranational organizations) or other social groups (communities of immigrated people, refugees, etc.) from the selfish appeals that guarantee the economic future of 'our people only', which means, in the end, returning to some strict autarchic doctrines and to the classical precepts of producerism (Ivaldi & Mazzoleni, 2018).

4. Less 'catchy words'; more constructive interpretations. Renovating the research agenda on the sovereignism-populism linkage

There is a wide consensus on the centrality of the compound phenomenon which goes under the concept of *populism*. However, we may define populism – as an ideology, a strategy, a style, or something else – it remains a key concept to understand current political dynamics. The celebrated definition of *thin-centred ideology* provided by Cas Mudde (2004, p. 543), for instance, deals with something which is at the core of current political transformation everywhere. However, as the same author of this definition has stressed more recently (Mudde & Rovira Kaltwasser, 2012), it is really hard to recognize the evidence of an effective impact of populism in the actual democratic life, and it is easy to confuse it with a number of diverse, although connected, phenomena. As a result, the literature on populism often floats from one meaning to another, and the empirical study of comparative politics is not always ready to produce a systematic research agenda on causes and consequences of populism. The reflection on this issue is burning. The recent assessment by Rooduijn (2019) emphasizes the problem of conceptual blurriness and the consequent risk of 'wrong conclusions' which may be evident from the blooming literature on populism in the years to come: As Rooduijn says ' ... For many scholars the sexiness of populism is an incentive to employ the term even if the real focus is on a different topic' (2019, p. 8).

I could not agree more. This is indeed the reason why this special issue has assembled a handful of articles, covering a wide range of research questions, while all addressing the populism-sovereignism linkage. I have tried to summarize some of the findings emerging from these articles, and I have extracted a few theoretical implications, in the attempt to limit the potential application of a general notion of populism and to use, conversely, the upstream multidimensional concept of sovereignism. In short, (at least) four dimensions can be explored in order to produce comparable empirical measurements of national, cultural, illiberal-personalized and economic sovereignism.

This is of course just a brief and still inaccurate attempt of assessment. But the feeling is that we are on the right track. If the goal of the special issue was to demonstrate that 'populism frames its political discourse in terms of recovery of a lost sovereignty' from globalized and allegedly unresponsive elites, we can say that the findings and the implications I have briefly reported clearly show that the intuition was right: the sovereigntist claims are, indeed, the most recurrent arguments in the construction of populist thin-centred ideology and they represent the *leitmotiv* in the discourse of many populist. But the distribution of these different *shades* of sovereignism among different types of players and in the different moments of the democratic life makes a systematic work of assessment particularly difficult. For this reason, I argue that we should take a closer look at the whole set of levels of analysis that we have to seriously consider, in the study of the present political change in Europe.

The first suggestion is to avoid paying all our attention to the unit 'political party' when we are trying to study the populist drift all around Europe. This is somehow connected to the results of a whole stream of seminal works produced in the past, but even the recent literature on populism shows the same limit: the assessment by Rooudijn above mentioned (2019), for instance, is a very stimulating discussion about the challenges to populist research. However, its empirical target is entirely centred on the empirical literature on political parties. Leaders – especially leaders of personalized, flash or even 'movement parties' (Della Porta, Kouki, & Mosca, 2017) – can be considered as rather autonomous key actors who transform the spread and transversal 'dissident voices' in a truly populist player. We have therefore to complement the typical observation on the side of political supply (for instance the analysis of party manifestos) and that on the demand side (for instance the public opinion surveys) with a systematical analysis of the plurality of views within the ruling class and by monitoring the degree of cohesion between leaders and party representatives.

Secondly, I would invite considering the long term and changing political strategies of sovereigntist/populist actors. The construction of new institutions, new public policy agendas and new types of coalitions are constrained by their capacity to gain reputation and by their problem-solving capabilities. The problem of the diverse approach of populist actors once they are in power is certainly not a new issue (Albertazzi & McDonnell, 2015) but a systematic empirical analysis of their institutional behaviour is missing: with this assertion, I mean an exhaustive effort in comparing the behaviour of these players in a number of 'usual' prerogatives of the political actors in government: patterns of coalition strategies, more or less policy-oriented ambition of portfolio allocation, policy advocacy and 'ministerial drifts' of the politicians who are delegated and individual attitudes to conflict/cooperation with other players. This has to do (also) with the issue of sovereignism, since a more comprehensive approach to the pattern of institutional behaviour would clarify if the economic sovereigntist claims of new left leaders/representatives/parties (for instance Syriza, Podemos or the Portuguese Bloco), 'anti-ideological movements' (Five Star Movement, or even the Greek ANEL for instance), ultra-conservative or far-right parties (the Norwegian FrP, the Austrian FPÖ, the Swiss SVP, the Italian League, not to mention the neo-nationalist parties from the Visegrad countries) follow effective strategies of empowerment for sovereigntist goals.

Finally, I would suggest paying more attention to the positioning on the typical sovereigntist issues of those political players – again, parties, leaders, representative elites and 'rulers' – who can clearly be labelled as 'non-populist'. Is an anti-populist stream currently at work in Europe? The issue is particularly hot since many leaders of the mainstream camp have recently employed political arguments and political styles often defined as populist: party personalization, the use of the 'people's sovereignty' against the bad attitudes of the 'elites', and others.

The empirical analyses of the multidimensional domain of sovereignism may be, in this respect, a fundamental test in the near future: are the European political leaders and the European political elites around them able to preserve some of the 'Weberian capabilities' as passionate, unbiased and professionalized rulers? And in case they aim at keeping their actions as 'transformative' leaders and 'responsible' elites, are they able to convince their followers of the benefits of a collaborative and integrative approach? In other words, do they shape a system of 'borders' with a design rationale in mind for the future of domestic democracy (and even in a supranational one, at least in the EU context), or do they simply claim for the National Interest and for the demand of people's sovereignty, just to provide a rhetoric response to the vocal demands arising from public opinion? Among the important themes to be analyzed in the near future, are the fundamental issues concerning the capability of the new leaders to speak true to their followers, and to stop systematically using fake news and media manipulation (Pajnik & Sauer, 2017).

I realize that this wide and somewhat ambitious agenda can be considered as a book of dreams, given the objective constraints to an extensive comparative study of all these features. Nonetheless, the questions at stake deserve a collective effort rather than the cultivation of a limited core group of super-specialists, like those who have had the merit to trace the roots in the study of contemporary populism. All the scholars of comparative politics and democratic institutions should be, therefore, interested in this new research agenda. They should feel part of a common collective effort, less 'creative' and less obsessed by the creation of new catchy taxonomies and definitions. They should be much more engaged with a common framework of relevant macro-phenomena to be explained in a truly *Rokkanian* tradition, and able to share data and empirical indicators to be used for the sake of a strong cumulative acquaintance. After all, this seems to be the main lesson we can receive from an accurate review of the populist-sovereigntist linkage: what we are talking about is something at the core of the dynamics of political change throughout the democratic hemisphere, and particularly within the group of European democracies.

ORCID

Luca Verzichelli 🅳 http://orcid.org/0000-0002-8159-5215

References

Abts, K., & Rummens, S. (2007). Populism versus democracy. *Political Studies, 55*(2), 405–424.
Albertazzi, D., & McDonnell, D. (2015). *Populists in power*. London: Routledge.
Caramani, D. (2017). Will vs. reason: The populist and technocratic forms of political representation and their critique to party government. *American Political Science Review, 111*(1), 54–67. doi:10.1017/S0003055416000538
de la Torre, C. (Eds.). (2019). *Routledge handbook of global populism*. London: Routledge.
Della Porta, D. J., Kouki, F. H., & Mosca, L. (2017). *Movement parties against Austerity*. Cambridge: Polity Press.
De Spiegeleire, S., Skinner, C., & Sweijs, T. (2017). *The rise of populist sovereignism: What it is, where it comes from, and what it means for international security and defense*. The Hague: The Hague Centre for Strategic Studies (HCSS).
Flinders, M., & Judge, D. (2017). Fifty years of representative and responsible government: Contemporary relevance, theoretical revisions and conceptual reflection. *Representation, 53*(2), 97–116.
Heinisch, R., Holtz-Bacha, C., & Mazzoleni, O. (Eds.). (2017). *Political populism. A handbook*. Baden-Baden: Nomos Verlag- Bloomsbury.
Hobolt, S. B., & de Vries, C. E. (2015). Issue entrepreneurship and multiparty competition. *Comparative Political Studies, 48*(9), 1159–1185.
Ivaldi, G., & Mazzoleni, O. (2018). *Economic populism and producerism. European right-wing populist parties in a transatlantic perspective*. Paper presented at the Seminar *El Populismo. Teoría y Experiencias contemporáneas*, University of Guadalajara.

Kallis, A. (2018). Populism, sovereigntism, and the unlikely re-emergence of the territorial nation-state. *Fudan Journal of the Humanities and Social Sciences, 11*(3), 285–302.

Mair, P. (2014). *Ruling the void*. London: Verso.

Moffit, B. (2016). *The Global Rise of Populism*. Stanford: Stanford University Press.

Mudde, C. (2004). The populist zeitgeist. *Government and Opposition, 39*(4), 541–563.

Mudde, C. (2007). *Populist radical right parties in Europe*. Cambridge: Cambridge University Press.

Mudde, C. (2016). *The study of populist radical right parties: Towards a fourth wave* (Working Paper No. 1) (pp. 1–23). Oslo: University of Oslo.

Mudde, C., & Rovira Kaltwasser, P. C. (2012). Populism and (liberal) democracy. In C. Mudde, & C. R. Kaltwasser (Eds.), *Populism in Europe and the Americas: Threat or corrective for democracy?* (pp. 1–26). Cambridge: Cambridge University Press.

Mueller, J. W. (2016). *What is populism?* Philadelphia: Univeristy of Pensilvania Press.

Pajnik, M., & Sauer, B. (Eds.). (2017). *Populism and the web. Communicative practices of parties and movements in Europe*. London: Routledge.

Pirro, A. (2014). Populist radical right parties in Central and Eastern Europe: The different context and issues of the prophets of the Patria. *Government and Opposition, 49*(4), 600–629. doi:10.1017/gov.2013.32

Pirro, A. L., Taggart, P., & van Kessel, S. (2018). The populist politics of Euroscepticism in times of crisis: Comparative conclusions. *Politics, 38*(3), 378–390. doi:10.1177/0263395718784704

Rooduijn, M. (2019). State of the field: How to study populism and adjacent topics? A plea for both more and less focus. *European Journal of Political Research, 58*(1), 362–372. doi:10.1111/1475-6765.12314

Rovira Kaltwasser, C., Taggart, P., Ochoa Espejo, C., & Ostiguy, P. (Eds.). (2017). *The Oxford handbook of populism*. Oxford: Oxford University Press.

Taggart, P., & Szczerbiak, A. (2004). Contemporary Euroscepticism in the party systems of the European Union candidate states of Central and Eastern Europe. *European Journal of Political Research, 43*(1), 1–27.

Tormey, S. (2015). *The end of representative democracy*. New York: Wiley.

Urbinati, N. (1998). Democracy and populism. *Constellations, 5*(1), 110–124.

Urbinati, N. (2014). *Democracy disfigured. Opinion, truth and the people*. Cambridge: Harvard University Press.

Van Kessel, S. (2015). *Populist parties in Europe: Agents of discontent?* Basingstoke: Palgrave Macmillan.

Verzichelli, L. (2018a). Degradable elites? Modes and factors of parliamentary turnover in Europe in the early twenty-first century. In L. Vogel, R. Gebauer, & A. Salheiser (Eds.), *The contested status of political elite: At the crossroad* (pp. 87–107). London: Routledge.

Verzichelli, L. (2018b). Elite circulation and stability. In H. Best, M. Cotta, J. P. Daloz, J. Higley, U. Hoffmann-Lange, J. Pakulski, & E. Semenova (Eds.), *The Palgrave handbook of political elite* (pp. 573–592). London: Palgrave.

Wilkin, P. (2018). The rise of 'illiberal' democracy: The orbánization of Hungarian political culture. *Journal of World-Systems Research, 24*(1), 5–42. doi:10.5195/JWSR.2018.716

Zakaria, F. (2007). *The future of freedom: Illiberal democracy at home and abroad*. New York: W. W. Norton & Company.

Index

Akkerman, A. 54
anti-establishment discourse 7–8
anti-sovereignist claims 22, 24, 83
Austrian Freedom Party (FPÖ) 14–16, 18–19, 21–22, 24–25, 28–30, 53, 56–59, 61–62
Austrian People's Party (ÖVP) 14–16, 18–19, 21–22, 24–27, 29–30; voters 25–28, 30
Austrian sovereignty 19, 22, 28–29

Bannon, Steve 38
Basile, L. 10, 71
Borri, R. 10
Brexit 4, 38, 61, 69–72, 74–75, 77–83
British party system 74

Cameron, David 75
Canovan, M. 54
Caramani, D. 115
civic sovereignism 77, 81–82, 111
conspiracy thinking 85, 88, 91, 94–95, 98–99
contemporary transformations 2
Craig, S. C. 93
Cronbach's alpha 91, 93
cue-taking hypothesis 90, 93
cultural sovereignism 36–37, 76, 87, 91, 94–95, 97–99, 111, 114
culture 7–8, 17, 36, 41, 45, 71, 87, 98, 109

denationalization 13, 28
dependent variables 39, 90–91, 94–95, 97, 99, 102
De Spiegeleire, S. 34
direct democracy 9, 19, 21, 27–28, 32, 34, 36, 38, 61, 82, 91
distinct concepts 6
domestic cultures 114
domestic economic policies 116

economic policies 16, 52–54, 62, 64, 87
economic populism 52–58, 62–64
economic populist sovereigntism 56–57, 64
economic populist sovereigntist themes 58
economic sovereigntism 52–57, 61–64

economic sovereignty 7, 14–15, 21, 24, 29–30, 55, 69, 73
Ennser-Jedenastik, L. 52
European radical right-wing populist parties 52
Euroscepticism 6, 14, 17, 33, 36, 71–72, 74

Gerring, J. 56
globalization 3, 8, 13, 16, 28, 33, 37, 56, 61, 86–87, 91, 109, 116

Habersack, F. 10
Heinisch, R. 10
Held, D. 3, 10
Hooghe, L. 37

individual determinants 85

Kallis, A. 5, 7–8
Kaltwasser, Rovira 5
Kitschelt, H. 16, 53
Kriesi, H.-P. 87

labour market mobility 17
leadership 59, 73–75, 114–115

Maastricht treaty 72–73
Maggiotto, M. A. 93
Mair, Peter 115
Marks, G. 37
Mazzoleni, O. 71
McGann, A. J. 53
McGrew, A. 3, 10
Meijers, M. J. 17
Mény, Y. 54–55, 62
Mitterlehner, Reinhold 24
Mudde, C. 53–54, 112, 117
Mueller, J. W. 112
multidimensional concept 7, 10, 86, 90, 94, 99

national sovereignism 7, 16–17, 77, 82
national sovereignist claims 22, 73
national sovereignty 5–6, 13, 15–19, 22, 56, 58, 60–61, 63–64, 69, 72, 108–109, 114–115

nation-states 2–5, 8, 33, 35–36, 48, 53, 62, 71
nativism 52, 54, 59

obsession effects 114
Otjes, S. 54, 57

people's sovereignty 62, 85–86, 109, 118–119
personalized illiberal democracy 114
political actors 4, 9, 13, 15, 47, 85–87, 109, 111, 114, 118
political economy 7, 52–54, 63
political parties 10, 17, 56–57, 75, 90, 118
political sovereignism 39, 87, 91, 94–95, 97–99, 115
popular sovereignism 15–16, 30
popular sovereignty 6, 8, 14–19, 21–22, 24–25, 28–29, 36, 38, 61, 97, 99
populism-sovereignism linkage 108, 110, 117
populist actors 6, 8–10, 15, 110–111, 113, 118
populist discourse 5–7, 9, 15, 70, 86–88, 109–110, 113–114
populist parties 7, 9–10, 64, 85–86, 90, 93, 99, 112
populist sovereignism 77, 82, 90
principal factor analysis 102
principled sovereignism 35–36
producerism 62–63, 116–117

radical right-wing economic sovereigntism 55
radical right-wing populist parties (RRPPs) 52–55, 57–58, 62–64
representative democracy 2, 5–6, 8–10, 71, 86, 94, 97–98, 111, 115–116
representative elites 114, 118
research contributions 9
research design 10, 75
responsiveness 89, 115

right-wing populism 6, 33, 35–36, 63
Rooduijn, M. 112–113, 117–118
Rovira Kaltwasser, C. 112

Schmidt, V. 73
Schumacher, G. 17
Seawright, J. 56
sovereignism-populism linkage 9, 110–112, 117
sovereignist claims 2–3, 6–10, 14–17, 22, 24, 26–27, 30, 71, 79, 82–83, 86, 89–91, 93, 97, 99
sovereignist retrenchement 95
sovereignist supporters 85, 98–99
sovereign people 5, 85, 87–89, 91, 93, 99, 115
sovereignty: claims 6, 15, 19, 21–22, 24–26, 29, 60, 63, 87–88, 99, 109; dimensions of 7, 19, 24–25, 29–30, 87
Surel, Y. 54–55, 62
Swiss People's party (SVP) 111
Switzerland 32–34, 38–39, 45, 57, 59, 61, 111, 114

Taggart, P. 56
Trump, Donald 34, 37, 47

UK Independence Party (UKIP) 5, 53, 56–59, 61–62, 74–75, 82
Urbinati, N. 8–9

Van Kersbergen, K. 17
Verzichelli, L. 10

welfare: abuse 17; chauvinism 52, 54–55, 63
Werner, A. 10

Zaslove, A. 56